Daring to
DANCE
with God

Daring to DANCE with God

Stepping Into God's Embrace

JEFF WALLING

Foreword by MAX LUCADO

HOWARD®
PUBLISHING CO.
West Monroe, Louisiana

Our purpose at Howard Publishing is:

- *Increasing faith* in the hearts of growing Christians
- *Inspiring holiness* in the lives of believers
- *Instilling hope* in the hearts of struggling people everywhere

Because He's coming again

Daring to Dance with God
© 1996 by Howard Publishing Co., Inc.
All rights reserved

Published by Howard Publishing Co., Inc.
3117 North 7th Street, West Monroe, LA 71291-2227

Printed in the United States of America
Third printing 1997

Cover Design by LinDee Loveland
Manuscript editing by Philis Boultinghouse

Library of Congress Cataloging-in-Publication Data

Walling, Jeff, 1957-
    Daring to dance with God : stepping into God's embrace / Jeff Walling.
      p. cm.
    ISBN 1-878990-55-1 (alk. paper)
    1. God—Worship and love. 2. Intimacy (Psychology)—Religious aspects—Christianity. 3. Walling, Jeff, 1957- . I. Title.
BV4817.W35 1996
248.4—dc20   96-13464
                                           CIP

Dedication

✦

To the people who taught me
to trust in a God I could not see
and live for a Savior I've never met—
my parents, T. J. and Mildred Walling

To the lady who showed me
what God's love looks like up close—
my ever patient wife, Cathryn Walling

To the three boys God is allowing me
to introduce to him,
Taylor, Riley, and Spencer Walling

Contents

✦

Foreword . . . . *xi*
Acknowledgments . . . . *xiii*
Introduction *1*

✦

SECTION ONE

An Invitation to the Dance
5 Steps Every Dancer Should Know

O N E – *page 9*
Giving up Yesterday's Baggage
STEP ONE: Letting Go

T W O – *page 23*
Finding the Faith to Hold On
Step Two: Taking His Hand

T H R E E – *page 39*
Submitting to His Will
Step Three: Following His Lead

F O U R – *page 53*
Committing Your Soul to Celebration
Step Four: Choosing to Rejoice

F I V E – *page 67*
Dancing on Thin Air
Step Five: Seeing the Invisible

✦

SECTION TWO
Overcoming a Handful of Excuses
5 Diseases That Stop the Music

S I X – *page 85*
Bethesda Blight – The Coward's Paralysis
Can't Dance, Don't Ask Me!

S E V E N – *page 99*
Marthaplexy – The Workaholic's Twitch
Can't Dance with My Apron On

E I G H T – *page 111*
Simonosis – Rigor Mortis of the Spirit
My Shoes Are Too Tight

N I N E – *page 125*
Nazaritis – Coma of the Soul
Too Bored to Bop

T E N – *page 141*
Michalepsy – The Critic's Blindness
What, Me? Do That?

Contents

✦

SECTION THREE
Learning to Dance When It Hurts
3 Special Dances for Painful Times

ELEVEN – *page 159*
Doing the Sinner's Tango
Beyond the Shame Game

TWELVE – *page 171*
Dancing in the Dark
When Things Go Really Wrong

THIRTEEN – *page 189*
Save the Last Dance for Me
Facing the Final Fight

And the Dance Goes On *203*

Foreword

✦

If you're intrigued by the title of this book—("My, a dance with God? How?")—then you should read it. The dance is God's idea—he'll lead you.

If you're bothered by the title of this book—("Humph, a dance with God? Heresy!")—then you should read it. The dance is God's idea—he invites you.

If you're intimidated by the title of this book—("To dance with God? He'd never ask me.")—then you should read it. The dance is God's idea—he awaits you.

Most of us have never been too good at dancing. Most of us relate to the folks on the edge of the party envying the folks on the floor: "They look like they're having so much fun, but *me*, oh, no, I couldn't."

And so we sip punch until time to go home. And we miss the waltz of our lives.

That's why Jeff Walling's work is so welcome. Let me tantalize you with my favorite paragraph of the book.

> And what is it like to dance with him?
>
> Dancing with God is allowing him to take our breath away as he whirls us through the dark and light places that life leads us. It is relaxing into his embrace and trusting fully in his strong arms. It is releasing the power of the Spirit within us to give us joy beyond measure. It is reveling in the unexpected and celebrating the divine surprise that is each new day. It is rejoicing out loud at the grace and beauty God provides and ignoring the calls of the crowd to sit down and quit grinning.
>
> But above all else, dancing with God is learning to let go.

What a delightful addition to our plodding faith are the words of Jeff Walling. This book is long overdue. Read it, and read it with delight. As you read, take note, you may sense your foot tapping to the music.

Max Lucado

Acknowledgments

✦

"As iron sharpens iron so one man sharpens another."

This book could not have been written without the support and encouragement of many fellow believers who've shaped my dance with the Lord. The following deserve special recognition:

My church family at Mission Viejo, who have helped me grow in countless ways and gave me three months in England to write and renew myself.

Our friends in England, whose Christian love gave our stay a double blessing.

Leon, Dave, Doug, Bob C., Bob J., Ray, and Hugo true shepherds who have prayerfully guided my ministry.

Rick and Agnes, a team whom I have been blessed to count as friends and coworkers for more years than either of us wish to acknowledge.

Patti, my ever faithful secretary who screens my calls, protects my time, and keeps me smiling.

Max Lucado, for his inspiration, encouragement, and letting me call him friend.

Philis, my brave and supportive editor whose scalpel made this book better—and shorter.

The crew at Howard Publishing who were the *labor and delivery* ward for this baby.

My family, Cathryn, and the boys, who have given up many days with Dad or nights with a husband so that I could preach, teach, and write.

All of you who have said for fifteen years, "You need to write a book!"

And most of all, *my Lord* who, gave me all the above, and grace on top of that!

dance, *dans*—*movement in rhythm, especially to music; to leap, skip, as from excitement; move nimbly. Any of the many kinds of dance steps.*

✦ Introduction

Don't you want to dance?

I do. I want to be swept away on a cloud of music and laughter. I want to experience the sheer bliss of waltzing and gliding across the room to the sound of an orchestra in full swing. And not just with anyone. No, I want to dance with the one who invented dancing. I want to dance with God.

And guess what? He wants to dance with me.

And he wants to dance with you too.

This book is designed to help you hear and accept God's invitation. He's been offering it to any who will listen ever since Jesus paid the ultimate price on a hill outside Jerusalem.

But understand this: the dance to which God invites you is not one of the physical realm—moving your body is a snap compared to getting your spirit's movement in time with God's tempo—no, the dance to which this book is dedicated is a dance of the heart, a dance of the soul. It's a dance that will change your life.

What's that you say? You've never considered dancing with God!

Maybe you've been persuaded that real Christians don't dance, that walking with Christ means sacrificing passion. Maybe you've believed that fits of passionate praise or flights of spiritual bliss are fashionable only for new Christians or possibly for late-night prayer sessions at a revival.

Or perhaps guilt and duty have come like masked bandits and stolen your joy. While you sing "Will It Do, Precious Lord?" these thieves whisper that it won't. Armed with *ought*s and *should*s they drive many into quiet desperation. Who among us has not lain awake wondering, "If only I had done more . . . "? After all, how dare we spend a moment smiling and dancing while others are dying lost? "Be ye joyful always" ends up being retranslated as "Grin and bear it till Jesus comes."

Or possibly you're just plain scared. Exuberant expressions of praise and joy can rock a good, conservative Christian back on his heels. And abuses of our freedom in worship have convinced some believers that the Puritans were right: too much celebrating of God's goodness turns the spiritual brain to mush. Every *Hallelujah!* is another step on the path to "sloppy agape" and "cheap grace."

Those obstacles are familiar to me too. For a time they kept me from accepting his exciting invitation. Yet, late at night, in the quiet of my heart, I couldn't stop wondering if there wasn't something more—something fuller, richer, and deeper.

For a while I accepted my misery quietly and put aside any dreams of dancing with God as fantasy. Don't pity me for this. You see, I had no idea how miserable I was. If you had asked about my burden, I would have responded like the country mule who, when asked by the city mule how he stood the weight of the huge pack on his back, replied, "What pack?" After all, few around me seemed to have any more joy than I. And the few who did were suspect. They obviously didn't know that Christianity was serious business.

But praise God for good news: the fruit of the Spirit is still joy. And we can and should experience it every day. What a relief to know that we are not called to be miserable! If real joy is not vibrantly alive in your faith each day, it's time you protest. If you have shared the feeling that there must be something more to your faith, take heart and read on.

But before you flip to the table of contents and look for a chapter called "How to Get Happy Fast," understand that no quick-fix formula for happiness can ever bring the depths of spiritual joy that Paul describes as "peace that passes understanding." Spiritual freedom and renewal can only come through the power of the Spirit. God must be given free reign in our hearts to relight the flame and rekindle our delight. Only he can transform a religious routine into a joyous ballet.

And he will only do it on his terms and at his tempo.

He demands that we open ourselves to the unexpected, the unpredictable, and even the unexplainable. The Bible is full of instances where God chose to work in outrageous and shocking ways: Walls fell down. Water stood up. Bread sprang from the ground. And the sun stood still.

And the days of his surprises are far from over.

So if you have grown accustomed to an orderly and predictable Christianity, I understand that turning the God of all creation loose within you can be an unsettling concept. But trust him. As Jesus said, he will not give you a snake if you ask for a fish.

Whether the well of your soul has been dry for a long time or you just want a little more passion in your piety and spring in your step, renewal and refreshment are available if you will take time to seek them. I pray that the simple biblical principles and steps you'll find in this book will help you venture out onto the dance floor and into his arms.

I have divided this book into three sections. The first shares the five basic steps of celestial dancing. This may be especially helpful to those who feel they've never experienced the depth of God's presence. Section two prescribes cures for five spiritual diseases that can steal your joy and hinder your dance. Those who've been sidelined by guilt, tradition, pride, or fatigue will find healing there. The final section addresses dances for the most difficult times in our lives—those times when dancing with God seems virtually impossible. In short, the goal of this book is to open your eyes to the daring possibilities and the wonder of dancing with God. Take it as a gentle nudge, urging you onto the floor, encouraging you to take those first awkward steps. Soon you'll be swirling and twirling to the various rhythms of life in the security of his arms.

So go ahead. Step into his embrace. He doesn't want us to be miserable. He just wants to dance . . . with you!

An Invitation to the DANCE

5 Steps Every Dancer
Should Know

"When in doubt, read the directions."

My brother-in-law, Sam, hates reading directions. The first thing he does after opening a Christmas present is to throw the instructions in the fireplace. "If it's too complex for me to figure out, I don't want to mess with it." While I admire his spirit, his aversion to reading about how part A fits into part B has cost him: there are more than a few gizmos lying around his house that still don't work.

Now, I understand that reading directions isn't normally much fun, but I think you'll enjoy the five steps you'll find in the following pages—for they are designed to lead you to unspeakable joy. You'll smile as you see how hard it is to let go and how important it is to know what to hold on to. You'll learn to follow God's tempo and trust his lead. And perhaps most important, you'll discover the power to celebrate, as you learn to see the invisible dance hall through which God guides you.

Yet no plan for personal change can be based on five easy steps or on grit and gumption alone. Christians often get treated like flesh-and-blood robots whose programming is corrected by simply introducing new data. "The Bible says rejoice, so do it!" If that were true, we could all change our lives by just knowing the right facts—"Don't diet, just read a diet book!" But dancing with God is an experience, not a theory. It is a lifestyle, not an event. Even the steps you'll find outlined here can't replace getting out there and trying it.

So, welcome to dance class. If you'll read the instructions and trust the Great Instructor, wondrous things lie ahead. Let's get to them.

You have turned . . . my mourning into dancing. You have put off my sackcloth and clothed me with joy.

✦ Psalm 30:11 NKJV

Giving up Yesterday's Baggage

STEP ONE:
Letting Go

I could not dance.

Well, that's really not true: I could dance, but I wasn't allowed to.

A prohibition against dancing was one of the many house rules that came with being raised in a preacher's family—not all preachers, mind you, but certainly the one I lived with.

My father, God rest his soul, had been a minister of the Gospel for longer than I could remember. My siblings and I were raised going to church every Sunday and Wednesday. I was probably the only kid in second grade with a three-piece suit and tie to match. Each Lord's Day, after we dressed, Mom would spread liberal doses of VO5 into my hair to give it that slick wave she thought so handsome. Then out the door to church we would go: my dad in his starched white shirt, my mom in her blue church dress, and my sister and I looking like perfect children—we were the Hallmark card family!

But conflict arose. My third-grade class was studying folk music, and as part of the curriculum on Wednesdays, we were to learn how to square-dance. It seemed innocent enough. Not ever having discussed this particular bit of American culture with my folks, I was unaware that it was on the "Momma-don't-allow-none-of-that-on-this-train" list. After dividing us into foursomes, the teacher would put on this recording of a hillbilly fiddler and try to get thirty eight-year-olds to follow directions. It was quite a sight. The worst part, of course, was the occasional order to "swing your partner!" This necessitated hand holding with the opposite sex, which was way out of the comfort zone of most third-grade boys. However, we giggled and struggled through it, trying to look as nonplused as possible. In truth, it was a lot of fun, especially when compared to a spelling test or multiplication table drill. The music and the rhythm, combined with the fun of just goofing around, made the whole thing quite pleasant.

But as you may imagine, that was not my mother's reaction. Again, not knowing any better, when Mom asked, "What did you enjoy at school today?" I put learning-to-square-dance at the top of the list. Her face quickly told me it would have been far better to have omitted that little bit of info. But it was too late. After grilling me for every detail, she informed me that she would have to talk with Dad about this. I knew what that meant.

At this point I must stress something: my mom and dad were great parents. They loved me and the Lord deeply and openly. They taught me about Jesus and deserve the lion's share of the credit for any good thing I have accomplished. However, there were a few areas in which their opinions were fixed. Dancing was one of them.

When my father learned of my transgression, he decided that it really had not been my fault. After all, I had not known better. I had not thought about the example I was setting. I had surely not considered the lust that such activities might incite. Now mind you, my parents did not try to discuss all this with me at the time. If they had, they might have discovered that at my age, when touching a girl, lust was considerably less a concern than cooties. But now that I knew better, the rule was clear: There would be no more dancing at school. The real problem was how to communicate this edict to my teacher. The wording of the note in a way that wouldn't cause undue embarrassment took some time. After several failed suggestions like, "We could just say he's very uncoordinated," they decided to be brief and to the point:

> Dear Mrs. Miller,
> Jefferson does not believe in dancing. Please excuse him from any further dancing at school.
> Yours,
> Mr. + Mrs. Walling

Armed with this little notice, I marched off to school the next day. Handing it to my teacher, I braced myself for her response. But all I got was a smile and "Oh . . . well, that's fine." I can only imagine what was said behind the teachers'-lounge door later that day. But Mrs. Miller never mentioned it again till the following Wednesday. When square-dance time rolled around, I was ready for mass embarrassment and was already practicing a limp to give myself a more socially acceptable alibi. But Mrs. Miller had her own plan. While the desks were being cleared away, she came up to me quietly and said, "Jeff, would you please operate the record player for me." A stroke of brilliance! I became the musical director for the class, putting the needle on and off at Mrs. Miller's command. Now *that* was good thinking.

As I settled into my new job, the sting of not being able to dance began to wear off. I would tap my foot and pretend to play the fiddle, while the rest of the kids stumbled through their *all-a-man left*s and *do-si-do*s. At home that day, I explained to my folks Mrs. Miller's brilliant idea. Thankfully, the theological ramifications of aiding and abetting sin were not raised, and my parents accepted this compromise as a reasonable way out.

So there I sat, week after week, watching everyone else dance and beginning to build what would become a deeply held conviction: real Christians don't dance.

Or smoke. Or drink. Or goof off. Or laugh in church . . . Go on, you finish the list.

You can thus imagine my surprise when years later, I read this account:

> *When those who were carrying the ark of the Lord had taken six steps, he sacrificed a bull and a fattened calf. David, wearing a linen ephod, danced before the Lord with all his might.* (2 Samuel 6:13–14)

There it was in big, bold black-and-white. One of the greatest men of all time—dancing! And not just dancing, but daring to dance "before the Lord." And as if that weren't enough, my jaw dropped even further when I spotted an interesting fact in the parable of the prodigal son. You remember the story of the wayward son who squandered his inheritance only to discover that there was "no place like home." But you may not have noticed what was going on at the party thrown in honor of his return: *"Meanwhile, the older son was in the field. When he came near the house, he heard music and dancing"* (Luke 15:25).

Now I've got to ask: *"Who* was in that house dancing?"

In a few verses we find out that it was none other than the prodigal's father. *"My son,"* the father explained to the older brother, *"we had to celebrate and be glad, because this brother of yours was dead and is alive again"* (Luke 15:31–32).

In the standard interpretation of this parable, the sons represent mankind and the father represents God himself. And if that's true . . . guess what? God is inviting us to come and dance *with him!*

Now there's a partner to line up for.

Just imagine! God invites us into intimacy with himself; he calls us into the celebration of all that's good and glorious. And he asks not that we stay at arm's length; rather he pulls us in tight, taking us for the dance of a lifetime.

And what is it like to dance with God?

Dancing with God is allowing him to take our breath away as he whirls us through the dark and light places that life leads us. It is relaxing into his embrace and trusting fully in his strong arms. It is releasing the power of the Spirit within us to give us joy beyond measure. It is reveling in the unexpected and celebrating the divine surprise that is each new day. It is rejoicing out loud at the grace and beauty God provides and ignoring the calls of the crowd to sit down and quit grinning.

✦

God wants to pull us in tight, taking us for the dance of a lifetime.

✦

But above all else, dancing with God is learning to let go.

We all discover early in life the importance of having something to hold on to—whether it is our mother's skirt or the handlebars of a Harley-Davidson. And when we hear, "Hold on tight!" our nerve endings begin to twitch. And my, can we hold on! We cling to control and security for all we're worth. We clutch power and property till our knuckles turn white. When danger threatens, we grab a gun or a girl or a glass of something strong and hang on till the storm passes. Hence, you can see the problem that arises when God invites us to dance with him. He holds out his hand and waits. The very act of taking his hand demands that we learn to let go of everything else. And three things in particular must be released before the dancing can begin.

✦ Letting Go of Fear

Experience is a stern but effective teacher. She has taught us well that you best keep one foot on the shore at all times. There are dragons out there—unexpected tragedies that can pop the balloon of a happy existence with the screech of a tire or the bang of a judge's gavel. "You can't go dancing off into tomorrow without a safety net and some good insurance," she chides. It's just not prudent.

Yet there God stands with his hand outstretched. He is calling us onto the dance floor with nothing more than a promise: *"Do not let your hearts be troubled. Trust in God; trust also in me"* (John 14:1).

Jesus makes it clear that we can *choose* whether or not to have troubled hearts. Worry and fear may feel involuntary, like the scream that erupts when the movie villain leaps from the shadows, but it is within our power to let go of our fear and take hold of the hand of God. "Do not worry" was the Savior's command to the disciples. There is no benefit found in it, unless gray hairs and sleepless nights are to be treasured. And while the positive health effects of not worrying are often discussed, the greatest motivator should be this: you cannot dance with God and cling to your fears. You can't enjoy the roller coaster if you're wondering whether the bolts will hold.

But there are those determined to try, poor souls who creep onto the dance floor and wince as they accept the divine invitation. For a time they may keep step with the Spirit, but soon their uneasiness overtakes them. They're the ones in church who look more like they are on their way to the dentist than to heaven. If you've tried dancing like this, you know why they wear those pained expressions: it's awfully uncomfortable to dance while looking over your shoulder.

But letting go of fear isn't a snap. Fear is a lot like gum: it sticks to your fingers. It can even be comforting in a perverse sort of way. There is a certain kind of pleasure found in sitting around and commiserating about one's deepest fears.

And where shall I put this fear if I *do* let go of it? The apostle Peter encourages us to put it in the only place that's fit—the Father's hand. *"Humble yourselves, therefore, under God's mighty hand, that he may lift you up in due time. Cast all your anxiety on him because he cares for you"* (1 Peter 5:6–7).

I have heard some use this verse to describe laying our burdens down at the throne of God. I've tried this, but I run into difficulties. You see, when I lay my burden at his feet, I have a strong tendency to want to *explain* it. I mean, he might not understand the depth of fear and frustration that this burden has given me. Soon, I have so vividly described the burden that I find I cannot leave it there. I just can't let go of it. So, I walk back out of the throne room still clutching my fear. That's why the word *cast* carries special importance for me.

The term is often used to describe hoisting a burden onto the back of an animal. Yet it also carries with it the notion of throwing, as casting a stone. When I come before the Lord, he doesn't simply bid me to *lay* my troubles down, he instructs me to *throw* them. That way, they are out of my hands for sure. Sometimes, the only thing that works is to just run into his presence, chuck my fears toward his throne, and dash back out before I change my mind.

And you know what? Not only is he a great dancer, but he can catch too!

✦ Letting Go of the Reins

The old cliché confirms that you can lead a horse to water . . . but that's a lot more than can be said for many of us humans. Though great leaders are highly praised and strong leadership is sought for country and community alike, there is an inherent problem with leading: it requires that someone follow. Maybe that's why Jesus selected his disciples with such simple instructions— "Follow me." If they would not submit to being followers, they would never be able to dance with God. Call it an eccentricity if you like, but God loves to lead.

This is no new requirement for God's followers. When Abram was summoned to leave all that he knew and trusted to become the father of the faithful, God didn't negotiate the route. Abram wasn't given a compass or map to guide him. He was asked to follow

God's lead, and he gladly handed God the reins. As the Hebrew writer put it, *"By faith Abraham, when called to go to a place he would later receive as his inheritance, obeyed and went, even though he did not know where he was going"* (Hebrews 11:8).

"*. . . even though he did not know where he was going.*" I love those words! They are so unashamedly honest. No pretense there. Think of it: Abram packed all his belongings and bade a tearful good-bye to his family. He hugged his brothers, Nahor and Haran, and kissed the hand of his father, Terah. At last he saddled up his donkey and set off for . . . where? Which way would he ride? We are told that he left without the slightest idea of where he was going. Yet he didn't seem too worried over how many pairs of underwear to take. He was just going to follow God. I don't know many of us who could have handled that one. After all, what would you tell the neighbors when they asked, "So, where you moving to?" Wouldn't you feel pretty foolish saying, "I haven't got the faintest idea!"

✦

Abram didn't seem too worried over how many pairs of underwear to take. He was just going to follow God.

✦

Yet that's when the dancing starts. The moment we truly abdicate the throne of our life and give God the control is the moment of discovery. It is then that we feel the joy and release found in not being in charge any more. We experience the peace and relaxation that come from having someone else at the wheel.

I know this feeling best from countless drives to the airport. I'm not one of those, you understand, who believes the travel agent's motto, "Always be there an hour before the flight." If I had been at the airport an hour before every flight I've taken, I would have spent half my life at LAX. So instead, I give my secretary ulcers by racing out the door at the last possible moment. And believe me, I know what the last possible moment is. I've timed the drive from my office to the airport down to the second. I can leave the drive-way fifty-seven minutes and twenty-eight seconds before a flight and still make it without a problem . . . most of the time.

Okay. Every now and then, something comes up—a traffic jam on the 5 freeway or an accident on the 405. And then I have to go into *hyperdrive*. My senses go on double alert as I watch for any break in the flow. I squeeze into the smallest niche in the traffic. I gauge the time that might be saved by taking side streets or crosstown freeways, and I dart down the off-ramp at the last second. Every minute feels like an eternity, and when I finally get to the airport, it's down to a foot race. A glance at my watch tells me that if I can get to gate 16 in 185 seconds, I can still catch the flight. It's doable . . . maybe.

I grab my overnight bag and sprint. Within the first hundred yards, my heart is racing, my chest is burning, and I'm kicking myself for bringing my laptop and my reading books! As I round the corner and dash through the metal detectors, I can see the gate in the distance. If it's really tight, I'll throw all modesty to the wind and start shouting, "Hold that flight; I'm coming!" By the time I get to the gate, my face is covered in sweat, and my arms and legs feel like lead. They rush me, breathless, down the ramp and close the plane door behind me. I collapse into the first available seat and . . . relax!

Foolish, isn't it? I'm about to be hurtling through the air at two hundred miles an hour in what amounts to an oversized Camp-bell's soup can, and I'm relaxing? Of course I am. And you know why: I'm not in charge anymore. While I was rocketing down the freeway, it was all up to me. Every decision lay in my lap. But now, it's all out of my hands. I'm not the pilot. I'm not going to worry about head winds or radar settings. I'm going to lean my seat back and let someone else worry. As President Truman is reported to have prayed each night, "Here's the country, Lord. I'm going to bed now. I'll pick it back up from you in the morning."

Only when you let go of the reins are you ready to dance. For with the freedom that releasing control brings, come the energy and drive to dance in celebration with the one to whom you've resigned the wheel. Just one more release remains.

✦ Letting Go of Guilt

Feeling guilty and dancing are mutually exclusive activities: you really can't enjoy them both at the same time. Dancing is joyous by nature. Oh, yes, there may be funeral dances done by natives on remote islands, but in the main, dancing is intertwined with celebration and exultation. Guilt, on the other hand, is depressing by nature. It is born of the knowledge of mistakes that were made and better choices that were missed. Thus, letting go of guilt must precede any attempt to join in the divine dance.

While letting go of guilt may sound much less unpleasant than letting go of the reins, an astonishing number of Christians find this the most difficult release of all. The difficulty may be rooted in our understanding of Christ's work.

During Jesus' life on earth, the only folks he seemed to have no time for were the self-righteous who thought they needed no savior. Seeing this, thoughtful Christians through the ages have agreed that avoiding self-righteousness is primary.

From ashes on the forehead to sackcloth on the body, believers have sought ways to keep their guilt before their eyes. Lamentably, these constant reminders of our need for God can easily mutate into an unhealthy focus on our own guilt. Hymn lyrics like "for such a *worm* as I" illustrate the depths to which we sink when highlighting our unworthiness.

But who wants to dance with a worm?

Clearly, we are guilty creatures. Without Christ, there is no hope for us. But this bad news is not where the curtain falls. God sent Christ to the earth to take the guilt of the world upon his shoulders. That means yours and mine. His blood on Calvary paid for all sins—big, small, past, present, and future. Imagine that—he has even paid for sins that we have not thought of committing yet!

Through this ultimate sacrifice, we are able, not only to stand before God guilt-free, but to join with him in celebration of that great truth.

Our guilt is released to the Father through the blessing of *forgiveness*. The very sound of that word should set our feet to tapping. It is the sweetest note of all: my slate is clean, and I am free. Unfortunately, many miss the double blessing of God's forgiveness. They focus solely on the fact that God has wiped away their sins. But David knew there was another miracle to be relished. When composing his own hymn about past guilt, presumably from his dalliance with Bathsheba, the psalmist put it this way:

> *Blessed is he*
> > *whose transgressions are forgiven,*
> > *whose sins are covered. . . .*
> *When I kept silent,*
> > *my bones wasted away*
> > *through my groaning all day long. . . .*
> *Then I acknowledged my sin to you*
> > *and did not cover up my iniquity.*
> *I said, "I will confess*
> > *my transgressions to the Lord"—*
> *and you forgave*
> > *the guilt of my sin.*
> > > (Psalm 32:1, 3, 5)

Now there's something to sing about! David rejoices in the hidden blessing of forgiveness: not only did God forgive the sin, he forgave the guilt as well. How else could the singer of Israel go on to praise his God so powerfully? He was not burdened with past guilt. He didn't carry the black bag around his neck, for he had let go of his guilt. He had allowed God to take it from him.

Will you allow God to take your black bag? I know you are unworthy of such a blessing, but go ahead anyway. Let go of the guilt that you have carried for years—maybe even decades. And while you're at it, how about handing over your fears too. They're so cold to the touch, anyway. And what about those reins? Come on. Don't make him pry your fingers off of them. Let them all go . . . you'll dance much better without them. Besides, you'll need your hands empty to take hold of his.

Now, won't you try it. Allow yourself to be swept along by the music of his dance, and take this first step to its wonderful rhythm. Let go . . . one, two . . . let go . . . three, four . . . that's it, you're catching on. But before you go flying too far across the floor, let's take a look at what you need to hold on to, for this promises to be one amazing dance.

Where can I go from your
Spirit?
Where can I flee from your
presence?

If I go up to the heavens, you are there;
if I make my bed in the depths,
you are there.

If I rise on the wings of the dawn,
if I settle on the far side of the sea,
even there your hand will guide me,
your right hand will hold me fast.

✦ Psalm 139:7–10

Finding the Faith to Hold On

STEP TWO:
Taking His Hand

Remember the old tune from the '70s—"Put Your Hand in the Hand of the Man Who Stilled the Water"? It's appropriate here, for the second step in daring to dance with God is to take his hand. Unfortunately, the very symbol of the hand of God may need some clarifying and defining. Through the years it has picked up some baggage we may need to jettison—though it came from some pretty respected sources.

Jonathan Edwards is one of those names that every aspiring preacher learns to hold in awe. His fiery expounding of God's Word marked him as one of the great gospel orators of the twentieth century. And his expounding had a good deal of *pound* in it.

His lessons were often grippingly emotional, painting pictures of the afterlife designed to scare the unrighteous into obedience. Possibly the most effective of these is a jewel titled "Sinners in the Hands of an Angry God." In it, Edwards depicts the judgment day, complete with the hoard of humanity waiting for God to assign them a final dwelling. One illustrator, in preparing a cover for the pamphlet printing of the sermon, sketched a pair of huge hands holding tiny helpless figures above what appears to be a giant barbecue pit. Sort of an eighteenth-century version of the "Turn or Burn" T-shirt. The illustration so caught the imaginations of the public that it, as well as the sermon, became a classic.

While I am convinced that many people may have been moved to consider their souls' salvation by images like these, the end result may not have been what either Edwards or God desired. If the thought of a sinner being in the hand of God carries with it more visions of judgment and fear than dancing and celebration, you can see how this might keep folks from reaching out to him.

Jesus paints quite a different picture of God's hands. According to him, there is no better place for sinners than in the hand of God.

> *My sheep listen to my voice; I know them, and they follow me. I give them eternal life, and they shall never perish; no one can snatch them out of my hand. My Father, who has given them to me, is greater than all; no one can snatch them out of my Father's hand.* (John 10:27–29)

Jesus assured his followers, and all else who would hear his words, that once in the hand of God, they were secure. No sneaky sheep thief could "snatch" them away from him. In short, sinners were safest in the place many have come to fear: the hand of God.

It is to this place that God calls any who would dance with him. Before we can celebrate our life with confidence, we must place ourselves, sin and all, in the hand of God. But don't let this picture of peace and safety, of security and protection, lull you into the notion that the hand of God is some great celestial easy chair—

always soft, comfy, and reclined. No, the hand of God is far too versatile to be pigeonholed like that.

What, then, will you find when you come to the hand of God? *It all depends on what you need.* Like the hand of any good father, his hand will provide just what you need when you need it. None may have understood this better than David. He uses the image of the hand of God nearly fifty times throughout the psalms to demonstrate the broad range of God's power and care. Let's look at these four and see which one you may be in need of right now.

✦ The Secure Hand of God

Ever want to run away? You know, just jump in the car and take off for good—head down the highway and leave it all behind. David understood that desire. That's why I call Psalm 139 his "run-away psalm." In it, he vents his frustrations about God's omnipresence, his "everywhereness."

> *Where can I go from your Spirit?*
> > *Where can I flee from your presence?*
> *If I go up to the heavens, you are there;*
> > *if I make my bed in the depths, you are there.*
> *If I rise on the wings of the dawn,*
> > *if I settle on the far side of the sea,*
> *even there your hand will guide me,*
> > *your right hand will hold me fast.*
>
> (Psalm 139:7–10)

While at times we all may wish we could "flee" from God's presence, David declares that there's no place to run from the God who is everywhere. He knows our thoughts before we speak and our plans before we make them. He sees in the dark and cannot be escaped. But in this seemingly fatalistic realization, David finds a wonderfully comforting truth: The same God who knows everything and is everywhere will hold me and guide me, no matter where I am. *"Your right hand will hold me fast."* How good it is to know that we are never far away from his guiding hand!

But how difficult it can be to accept the places that hand leads us. As long as it's beside the still waters and in the green pastures, I'm glad to be guided, but when he takes me into more dangerous territory, my confidence level drops. I become like a dog who realizes he's being taken to get shots: it's a battle just getting me in the car! David uses a similar image to describe his own reluctance to being guided by God in Psalm 73:22–24.

> *I was senseless and ignorant;*
> *I was a brute beast before you.*
> *Yet I am always with you;*
> *you hold me by my right hand.*

Like a donkey who refuses to move, David recalled times when he had balked at God's leading. Yet he assures us that the divine hand is ultimately leading us to joy. At no point in the journey are we abandoned: *"I am always with you; you hold me by my right hand."* Those words always bring back memories of the beach and the summers when I learned to swim.

We didn't live far from the ocean, but going there was still a rare treat. My mother wasn't a "water person," as she liked to say, but at least twice each summer my dad would convince her to go anyway. On those Saturdays the whole family would pile into our blue Ford station wagon, equipped with plastic sand shovels and picnic basket, and head for the coast. Mom would spread out a blanket and get sun lotion on us all, and my father would check out the water. I don't know why he felt the need to "check it out." It was always miserably cold, I thought, even on the hottest day of summer. So when he'd yell, "The water's great!" I would stick to my sand-castle building and let my other siblings go freeze with him. Actually it wasn't just the cold: not being around water much, I had never learned to swim. To me, the crashing waves of the blue Pacific looked like "death by water." But Dad wouldn't let it go. After swimming with my sister awhile, he'd trot back to the beach chairs, stick out his hand and say, "All right, son, come on." There was no refusing: I'd tried before. Glumly, I would take hold of that salty hand and head for the water.

The closer we'd get to the surf, the slower I would walk, and the tighter I'd squeeze. And by the time we were actually in the waves, I would be hanging on for dear life. Once I even offered him all my toys if we could just go back to the sand. I thought he was torturing me for kicks, but my Dad knew there was a lesson here I had to learn.

As the waves rose around me, so did my panic level. Soon, their force would sweep me off my feet, and for a few terrifying seconds, I would float loose in all that foam. Well, not really loose: I had my father's hand. No matter how hard the waves crashed around us, no matter how many times I felt my feet go flying, he never once let go. Eventually I would begin to relax and actually enjoy the experience. It seemed that was what he was waiting for. When I would begin to smile and even laugh, my father would say, "Okay, you want to go back now?" Go back? No way! This was just getting fun. And for the next hour, we would laugh and play in the ocean till we returned exhausted but happy to lay on the sand and soak up the sun.

Those memories are so much like the way God deals with us. He offers his hand, and we fearfully take hold. But our lack of faith and trust keep us from enjoying the water. What might happen tomorrow? What if it brings a really big wave? David reminds us that God's hand is strong and sure. There is no wave that can tear us from his loving grip. He will guide us through trackless seas and hold us fast while fear and loneliness try to knock us off our feet. And when choices perplex us and the best path seems impossible to find, his hand will gently lead us where we need to go. It is one of the great joys of dancing with him. As Paul puts it: *Those who are led by the Spirit of God are sons of God*" (Romans 8:14). God will always lead his people through his Spirit, if we will only take his hand.

27

✦ The Satisfying Hand of God

Though guidance is essential, God's hand does much more than just take us where we need to go. He provides what we need once we arrive. And what is it that you need? The range runs from food and clothing to self-fulfillment and personal growth. Can God's hand give all of this? Yes, and more. His hand can give the one thing every human seeks: *satisfaction*. Again David's words describe it well:

> *How many are your works, O Lord!*
> > *In wisdom you made them all;*
> > *the earth is full of your creatures.*
> *There is the sea, vast and spacious,*
> > *teeming with creatures beyond number—*
> > *living things both large and small.*
> *There the ships go to and fro,*
> > *and the leviathan, which you formed to frolic there.*
> *These all look to you*
> > *to give them their food at the proper time.*
> *When you give it to them,*
> > *they gather it up;*
> *when you open your hand,*
> > *they are satisfied with good things.*
> > > (Psalm 104:24–28)

Turning as he often does to nature, David points us toward the sea. Life there involves no planting or harvesting, no baking or boiling, no storing up wheat for the winter or grinding up corn for bread. Instead, all the creatures who inhabit the sea have only one place to turn for physical satisfaction—the hand of God. Without silos or barns, they must depend each day on the providence that God built into his creation—what David calls his hand.

And what does that hand do? It opens. That's it. And within it are found all that is needed for satisfaction. But you may protest,

28

"That may be fine for the fish in the sea, but what about me and my needs?" Look at a similar passage from Psalm 145:

> *The eyes of all look to you,*
>   *and you give them their food at the proper time.*
> *You open your hand*
>   *and satisfy the desires of every living thing.*
> *The Lord is righteous in all his ways*
>   *and loving toward all he has made.*
>
> (vv. 15–17)

Did you see you and I in there? "Every living thing." It seems we, too, are invited to line up with the perch and the marlin to get what we need from God. We are as dependent on his providence as the sparrow or the dolphin. Understand that David is not calling us to laziness or sloth—working is as much a part of our nature as swimming is for the creatures of the sea. But believing that it is our work or our planning that sustains us denies the place of God's hand. We must not become like the crusty old farmer who, when asked by the visiting preacher to give thanks before the meal, said, "God, I planted this corn, I picked these beans, and I raised that chicken. So thanks for nothing. Amen." A better refrain would be, "Without him, I am nothing." No matter what our role, it is God who provides what we eat, drink, and wear.

And he doesn't stop with food and shelter. God's hand will satisfy our deepest emotional and psychological needs for belonging and esteem. That elusive ghost, Personal Satisfaction, has lead many on a wild-goose chase. From bungee jumping to white-water rafting, people look everywhere for something that will fill the empty place inside, something that will satisfy.

For many, personal identity and self-esteem are inextricably tied to our notion of work. What are you? A teacher. A preacher. A farmer. A salesman. You are what you do: if you aren't doing something, you ain't nothing. If this thinking sounds unfamiliar, try going without a job for a few months and watch the effect. It's how I ended up working in a car wash for five weeks.

I had finished five years of service at one church as an associate minister and had accepted a pulpit position with another. I was scheduled to leave my first job at the end of the year, but at the request of my new wife, had postponed my new position's start date till March first. That gave me two months to relax and settle into marriage without the hassles of work. Sounds great, right? Those first few mornings as I waved good-bye to my wife as she headed off to work felt wonderful. I tinkered about in our new apartment. Put a light in here, hung a mirror there, and generally just took it easy. But that joy lasted about two weeks. I began to feel restless and abandoned as she would whisk out the door each morning. And when she'd return, I'd pump her for every detail of her day, anxious to hear any tidbit of news from the outside world. The last straw came when I proposed a weekend ski trip in February and she replied, "Well, I guess we can afford it—on just my paycheck." Her paycheck! I felt like a welfare case. All I needed was a poster of me captioned, "Please give money so this poor child can go to ski camp."

The next day, I took the car to be washed. At least I was doing something productive. Still fuming about the whole matter, I noticed a small sign: "Cashier Needed. Apply Here." You can guess the rest. I was so excited when Cathryn came home that evening—I could hardly wait for her to ask me about my day. "I got a job today," I tossed off as casually as I could.

"What do you mean?" she asked.

"I'm the cashier at the car wash down the street for the next five weeks. It pays $6.10 an hour, minus withholdings. I'll earn enough to cover the whole ski trip . . . your expenses and mine. It'll be my treat!"

When she finally stopped laughing and realized I was serious, she just shook her head. "Promise me you won't tell anybody," she said. And I promised her I wouldn't. So you keep this quiet, all right?

Isn't it amazing—the lengths we go to in trying to satisfy our need to be something, to accomplish something? Yet, when we place ourselves in God's hand, we no longer need to live off the approval of others or the accomplishments of our hands. He provides that all-important sense of satisfaction. His affirmation and approval secure our identity and satisfy our need to be someone. When this happens, work and career become part of life's dance—instead of life's duty.

If you are unsatisfied, if your heart aches with unfulfilled longing, if you're wanting, needing, something more, ask God to open his hand. Accept from him the secret of contentment that Paul told the Philippians he possessed: *"For I have learned to be content whatever the circumstances. I know what it is to be in need, and I know what it is to have plenty. I have learned the secret of being content in any and every situation, whether well fed or hungry, whether living in plenty or in want"* (Philippians 4:11–12). That kind of complete and constant satisfaction comes from only one source—the hand of God.

✦ The Disciplining Hand of God

While the Father's hand brings to mind countless images of security and guidance, it would be unfair to skip a less agreeable but equally vital function. Within David's psalms the hand of God is often an instrument of discipline and correction. Whether crushing the wicked with "his mighty hand" or delivering justice from his "powerful right hand," it is clear that the hand of God can be firm when needed. Again, David knew this from *firsthand* experience.

> *Blessed is he*
> > *whose transgressions are forgiven,*
> > *whose sins are covered.*
> *Blessed is the man*
> > *whose sin the Lord does not count against him*
> > *and in whose spirit is no deceit.*

When I kept silent,
my bones wasted away
through my groaning all day long.
For day and night
your hand was heavy upon me;
my strength was sapped
as in the heat of summer.

(Psalm 32:1–4)

Sin is gross. Every time I see its effects in my life or in the lives of those around me, that reality is confirmed. It always leaves pain and sorrow in its wake, without regard for age or station in life. But it is important to recognize that some parts of the aftermath of sin can be God's own doing. Notice David's language as he describes the pressure and guilt he carried while he tried to keep his transgression hidden. It was the *"hand of God"* that was *"heavy"* on him. It was God who took his strength and left him feeling as weak as one who has walked a long way on a hot day. Anyone who has felt the weight of sin and the depression that unresolved guilt can bring will relate to these feelings.

O Lord, do not rebuke me in your anger
or discipline me in your wrath.
For your arrows have pierced me,
and your hand has come down upon me.
Because of your wrath there is no health in my body;
my bones have no soundness because of my sin.

(Psalm 38:1–3)

But it can be troubling to realize that these pains come from God. Could his loving hand bring such hurt? You need only reflect on your youth to know the answer to that question. The same loving hand that held me up in the waves and provided food for my table would also whack my bottom when the occasion warranted. And the occasion often warranted. Only years later did I appreciate the value of those "manual lessons" when I began to apply them to my own children. As the wise proverb writer said, *"He who spares the rod hates his son, but he who loves him is careful to discipline him"* (Proverbs 13:24). Discipline is an essential function of the hand of God. Unfortunately, dodging that discipline is the natural reaction of man. Who hasn't tried to talk his way out of a spanking or two?

David was no different. He, too, tried to dodge the ache of guilt that God sent him. To be sure, guilt can cause problems in one's dance with God, as we discussed in chapter 1. But it also plays an important role in making sure we are dancing a righteous dance. In this sense, it functions like your body's nervous system—if you cut your finger while working in the garden, it hurts. That ache is trying to say, "Stop and deal with this." If you are pressed for time or just want to be tough, you'll try and ignore the ache—just wrap a handkerchief around it and keep working. But if the cut is deep enough, your marvelous nervous system won't let you ignore it. It will keep shouting louder and louder until you can't hear anything else over its piercing screams of, "Get this finger some help, *now!*"

When you're finally convinced that ignoring the ache is futile, you might try to silence it. "Maybe if I take a couple of aspirins, this stupid finger will stop hurting!" And for a time, this can be effective. Professional football players have been known to finish a game with a broken bone that they could not even feel thanks to the wonders of Novocain. But even though you muffle the messenger, the message is still true: you have a problem here, and you've got to deal with it. Ultimately, it may take gangrene to break through all your defenses and announce that the problem has gone from serious to critical. Sadly, at that point, the only solution left may be amputation.

So it is when we try to dodge a spiritual ache. Whether the problem is jealousy, deceit, bitterness, or sloth, the hand of God will begin to press on our spiritual nervous systems and send an ache. Sometimes it's an inner ache—thoughts and memories that just won't let go. They remind us of our unresolved sin. We may try to ignore that inner voice and just focus on other things. If that fails, we may try to numb the ache. Whether with a pill or a drink or a night out at the movies, we shoot a little Novocain in our hearts and forget the pain . . . for a while. But then the hand of God presses harder. He may bring pressure from the outside, circumstances that come to bear on us and motivate us to face the music. We come across an article in a book we're reading or a text in the Bible that fairly shouts at us—this is you! Friends call and say they've been worrying about us and don't know why. A skeleton we had carefully packed away in the closet comes bouncing out, and all of a sudden we are forced to face our problems.

> *Whether with a pill or a drink or a night out at the movies, we shoot a little Novocain in our hearts and forget the pain . . . for a while.*

If you consider David's path, he actually added more mistakes on top of his problem in the hopes of "fixing it." He tried lies, deceit, and even murder to stop the ache. And God just pressed harder until there was nothing David could do but deal with it. And only then did the hurting finally stop. Paul described it well to the Corinthian church:

> *Even if I caused you sorrow by my letter, I do not regret it. Though I did regret it—I see that my letter hurt you, but only for a little while— yet now I am happy, not because you were made sorry, but because your sorrow led you to repentance. For you became sorrowful as God intended and so were not harmed in any way by us. Godly sorrow brings repentance that leads to salvation and leaves no regret.* (2 Corinthians 7:8–11)

If the hand of God is pressing on you, don't dodge the ache. Put down the bottle of spiritual Darvon and embrace the pain. Look it full in the face and listen to its message. It may be just the ghost of an old sin you need to give to God again. But it may be an unresolved wrong that God is pressing you to deal with. Dancing with God demands that you face these aches so you can find the joyous release that comes through confession and forgiveness.

✦ The Restoring Hand of God

In the later years of David's life, I believe he came to appreciate one other function of God's hand more and more. This last, and possibly most tender, characteristic of the hand of God is expressed in Psalm 37:23–24.

> *If the Lord delights in a man's way,*
> *he makes his steps firm;*
> *though he stumble, he will not fall,*
> *for the Lord upholds him with his hand.*

In a world where walking was the number-one form of transportation, stumbling was a common problem. The country roads that David walked would have been little more than dirt paths. And the stone-paved streets of the cities weren't much better. Unlike the nice, smooth variety found at Disneyland, the cobblestone paths of David's day were made of rugged stones. The natural imperfections of these stones made walking even a few paces without your eyes glued to the ground a challenge. And just try running!

So when David painted a picture of his life's path, he never pretended that it was stumble free. The important question was, What happened after he stumbled? That's where the restoring hand of God came in. When an odd-shaped stone caught his foot and his balance began to go, the steadfast hand of the one who guided him just pulled him upright again. It's much like a child learning to ride a bike.

When our eldest son said he was ready for the training wheels to come off his bike, we knew it wouldn't be pleasant. But at his insistence, off they came. My wife stood on the lawn in front of our house as Taylor prepared for his maiden flight down the driveway *sans training wheels*. He sat upright on the bike and tested gravity a bit to see if the bike really would fall over. I could see the look of delight fade as he realized that once he began rolling down that slope, there would no longer be anything to keep him from going head to head with the pavement. He looked at me and said, "Dad, I think I'll fall."

"No, you won't." I lied through my teeth and then looked at my wife. Cathryn threw me a classic mother's look—her brow knotted, her hands wrapped together as if in prayer, and her eyes pleading, "Please, don't let my baby get hurt." I was about to tell her to go inside if she couldn't handle this, when I heard Taylor yell.

"Dad!!!" He was already sailing out of the driveway and onto the street. Miraculously, he was still more or less upright, but I could see the infamous front-wheel-wobble that signaled he was badly overcompensating for every bend in his path. His luck wouldn't hold, I knew, without some help. So off I ran, my fatherhood at stake. If he crashed, my son would never trust me again, and my wife would shoot me, then divorce me! But just as the bike was going into a terminal lean to the left, I caught the rear of his seat with my hand. The tragedy was averted. But now, if I stopped him dead in his tracks, he would be catapulted over the handlebars and so much for Father of the Year. So I just kept running. Applying barely enough pressure to keep him vertical, I trotted silently behind him to the end of the street, where he glided to the sidewalk and stopped, resting his left foot on the curb. "I did it, Dad!" he shouted. Only when he turned around to discover me huffing and puffing behind him did he realize that *we* had done it.

David says that God will go to even greater lengths to lift us up when we stumble, to restore us to an upright position when we fall. But, as always—only if we will take his hand. If, instead, we fall prey to an "I'd rather do it myself" mentality and seek to steer our own ship and handle our own hurts, then we block God from rescuing us. His strong hand waits for us to call out:

Reach down your hand from on high;
deliver me and rescue me
from the mighty waters,
from the hands of foreigners.

(Psalm 144:7)

Whether our stumble is due to negligence or disobedience, the Father is ready to reach out and put us back on our feet. All the while Satan whispers that we are not worthy of his touch and have no right to ask for restoration. This lie is as powerful as it is foolish. It's like suggesting that you clean up before you take a bath! Our weaknesses and mistakes are what sent Christ to Golgotha. If we do not freely bring them to the Father and allow him to renew our soul and restore our balance, we rob the cross of its power.

If your knees are bruised from stumbling and your shins are bloody from an unexpected tumble, don't let embarrassment or fear cause you to slink off into the bushes to mope. Reach out for the tender hand of one who knows and cares. He is aware of your every misstep and loves you anyway.

David knew the guiding, satisfying, disciplining, and restoring power of God's hand. He had felt its touch when things were dark as well as when the birds sang and the sun shone. And best of all, he knew that the God he worshiped loved him and wanted him to dance. So whether you need direction, nurture, correction, or rescue, put your hand in the hand of the one who stilled the waters. You'll find everything you need there . . . including the hole that the nail left.

O f what value is an idol, since a
man has carved it?
Or an image that teaches lies?

For he who makes it trusts in his own
creation;
he makes idols that cannot speak.

Woe to him who says to wood, "Come to life!"
Or to lifeless stone, "Wake up!"

Can it give guidance?
It is covered with gold and silver;
there is no breath in it.

But the Lord is in his holy temple;
let all the earth be silent before him.

✦ Habakkuk 2:18–20

Submitting to His Will

STEP THREE:
Following His Lead

"The Lord is in his holy temple, let all the earth keep silent before him."
That passage has probably appeared over more sanctuary doors than any other, but have you ever looked into its context? For many years I thought of those words only as the opening line of the famous hymn. In the church where I grew up, almost every Sunday morning service began with that song. It was an informal call to worship, often started by someone in the back of the audi-torium . . . *"The Lord is in his holy temple."*

As a child, I used to imagine that it was the notification that God had finally showed up for church, as though there were some deacon stationed at the door ready to cue the song leader when the Lord's car drove up. As I matured, it became obvious that one of the song's functions was to get everyone to sit down and hush up so that services might begin. At one point, bored by the monotony, some of my friends even invented their own lyrics to the tune—to be sung only under your breath, mind you:

> It's time to start church so shut up.
> It's time to start church so shut up.
> Shut up, shut up,
> Sit down and shut up.

You can imagine the giggles that rolled through the youth group from then on whenever the song was sung. Needless to say, we missed the point of the song, but I wonder if the rest of the congregation missed the point of Habakkuk's text. You see, the prophet didn't write those words to encourage reverence in worship services. He was addressing the problem of where people go for guidance and advice. Look at the words in their fuller setting:

> *Of what value is an idol, since a man has carved it? . . .*
> *Woe to him who says to wood, "Come to life!"*
>> *Or to lifeless stone, "Wake up!"*
> *Can it give guidance?*
>> *It is covered with gold and silver;*
>> *there is no breath in it.*
> *But the Lord is in his holy temple;*
>> *let all the earth be silent before him.*
>> (Habakkuk 2:18–20)

The people of Israel were looking to idols of their own creation instead of to the God of creation for their spiritual guidance. Rather than simply condemn this act, the prophet underlined the foolishness of their sin. "Who would be silly enough to carve a statue out of wood or chisel it out of stone and then bow before their own lifeless creation asking it for guidance?"

We would.

✦ In Search of Guidance

Whether to a computer or a Ouija board, mankind still looks to tools of his own design to decipher his destiny. Society boasts that technology holds all the answers and that soon we will control everything from our DNA to the power of interterrestrial travel. The mysteries of the ages will be unraveled by computers, we are told, and we will be able to hold the future itself right in our laptops. And, oh, our fascination with technology grows with every new gizmo.

On a trip to visit his family, a friend recently rented a luxury car in San Francisco and was asked, "Would you like one with a navigational guidance system?"

"What?" he asked. He was informed that the newest cars came with the option of a computer guidance system hooked up with a global positioning satellite that would actually talk to you! Since it cost only a few dollars more, he couldn't resist. Once behind the wheel, he decided to try it out on a familiar course. He punched in his father's home address, and the computer started speaking to him as he drove. "Go straight three more blocks and turn left." Can you imagine this? He even tried tricking the thing by pulling down a dead-end street and just sitting there. After a moment of silence the computer said, "Back up, please!"

What's next? Software is already available that will tell you how to guide your investments and manage your business. How far away is the program that will tell you how to fix your marriage and manage your emotional problems? Mind you, I'm not anticomputer at all—this chapter is being typed on one, with a spell-checker included!

But Habakkuk's warning is for us if we believe that we can say to a lifeless computer chip or semiconductor, "Which way should I go with my life?" The spiritual guidance we need will never be found in our inventions. Through Habakkuk's words God declares that no created thing can ever provide divine knowledge. But God doesn't leave us without a guidance system: If you really want to

41

get the facts from someone in authority, you know where to find him—*"The Lord is in his holy temple."* Go there, be silent, and he will give you guidance.

✦ A Divine Navigation System

Since the sin in the Garden, God has been in the process of returning mankind to relationship with him. Consider the path he took. In the days after Noah, the language of the Bible pictures God as living far from man. He would *"come down to see"* what man was up to (Genesis 11:5). This kind of language implies the great distance that man felt from God. And whenever God did confront man face to face, man was frightened and overwhelmed. When Jacob awoke from an encounter with God he cried out: *"'Surely the Lord is in this place, and I was not aware of it.' He was afraid and said, 'How awesome is this place! This is none other than the house of God; this is the gate of heaven'"* (Genesis 28:16–17). Even a moment's encounter with God was considered a privilege.

But then God took a step closer. Moses was called to Sinai, and when he came down with his face glowing and mind reeling, the news he brought was astonishing! Though the Ten Commandments grabbed the spotlight, the other significant news flash from the mountain was just as incredible: "God is coming to guide us personally!" He commanded that a beautiful tent of meeting be constructed. The Lord of heaven and earth, it appeared, wanted an apartment right in the middle of their neighborhood—or at least a mobile home! The tabernacle became not only the center of Jewish religious life but also the source of guidance for Israel. They never wondered where they should go next. When the cloud or fire above it moved, they simply followed. Talk about personal divine direction—they had it!

When the mobile tabernacle was replaced with the stationary temple of Habakkuk's day, it was the place to go to inquire of the Lord and seek his will. But God wanted to move his guidance system closer still to man. Through the miracle of the virgin birth, the Creator put on flesh and walked the dusty streets of Palestine in the body of Jesus of Nazareth. He offered humanity the kind of guiding relationship it had not had since the Garden: they could actually walk and talk with God. Once again God's people didn't have to ask which way they should go—their simple instructions were to "follow Jesus." They could hold his hand and hug his neck. No closer guiding relationship could have been dreamed of until . . . God came nearer still.

When Jesus left the earth, he promised that a counselor would come to guide his followers. *"But when he, the Spirit of truth, comes, he will guide you into all truth. He will not speak on his own; he will speak only what he hears, and he will tell you what is yet to come"* (John 16:13). Through the Spirit, God offered direction and guidance that come not from without but from within. We are invited to be "spirit-led" people, to dance with God by keeping *"in step with the Spirit"* (Galatians 5:25) who, as Paul says, *"is in you"* (1 Corinthians 6:19). Through this marvelous process he provides us with our own internal guidance system in the person of the Holy Spirit. I need only enter into prayer to enter the Holy of Holies where God waits to give me direction and reveal his will. As I read his word and as the Spirit works in my heart, I am guided in a closer way than Israel could have ever envisioned. I can actually reach out, take the hand of God, and accept his lead in the dance of life.

✦ Learning to Follow His Lead

So why is being led by the Spirit such a challenging and confusing thing for many believers? It may be that having taken his hand, we have trouble following his lead. I can't count the times I've heard questions like, "How do I surrender my will to his?" or "How do I let him have control?"

No one biblical writer addresses these questions more passionately and practically than Paul. He knew well the battle that ensues when any human tries to turn his life over to the Spirit. In the eighth chapter of his letter to the Romans, he gives us a marvelous picture of this process and offers at least three keys for letting it happen in our own lives.

Admitting the Need to Be Led

> *Therefore, there is now no condemnation for those who are in Christ Jesus, because through Christ Jesus the law of the Spirit of life set me free from the law of sin and death. For what the law was powerless to do in that it was weakened by the sinful nature, God did by sending his own Son in the likeness of sinful man to be a sin offering.* (Romans 8:1–3)

The beginning of following God's lead is an admission that we need leading. The law given on Sinai proved incapable of guiding man to righteousness because of what Paul calls the weakness of our *"sinful nature."* We cannot chart our own course because we are unable to recognize right from wrong. Since the Garden, each time man has tried to steer his own course, he has run off the road. Yet each time we fail, we convince ourselves that with some new information or better planning, we can overcome the obstacles and find our own way.

Even believers can fall prey to the foolishness of trusting some*thing,* instead of some*one,* to chart their path. When was the last time you looked over a brochure for a Christian time-management product or seminar? You know, those spiritual "Daytimers" that offer "a simple method of being where you need to be when you need to be there." Do you hear the arrogance in that promise? Yet we sign up, actually thinking that we can learn to prioritize our lists and chart our lives like engineers building a new spacecraft. You come back with a new notebook and a basketful of self-confidence. "I can take charge of my day!" says the little sticker I am advised to put on my desk. But all too quickly our carefully planned schedules collide with the wonderful randomness of life.

And then, confidence in shreds, we become irritated as our "To Do" list goes up in flames. We are sullen, guilt-ridden, and frustrated . . . until we spot the next "Get Yourself Organized" seminar, and off we go!

While I'm not condemning good organizational skills, Habakkuk would agree that they are no substitute for divine organization. God wants to take our scheduling pen in his hand, but only when we admit that we can't handle it on our own.

But once again, it is often my ego that stands between me and this all-important admission. Everything within me screams "failure" when I finally crumple up my "To Do" list and say, "God, I give up. I can't get it done." That's because most of us have bought into the image of the successful, self-directed, and confident Christian who knows where he's going and how he's going to get there.

But we will never be able to follow the lead of the Lord while believing we don't need his leading. Like a drowning swimmer who doesn't believe he's drowning, we can't be saved until we acknowledge our own inadequacy. And God refuses to force me to surrender. I must choose freely to do so, based on the knowledge that I am desperately in need of his hand on my rudder.

♦

All too quickly our carefully planned schedules collide with the wonderful randomness of life.

♦

If the Proverb writer was right when he said that it is not within man to guide his own footsteps, maybe we should quit pretending that it is. Try something new in the middle of your next personal planning session: stop and say, "God, I don't know how to do this. I need you to lead, here and now." What would be the result if every church in the world came to that very confession? Every Christian family? The comforting relief that courses through you when you admit you can't steer your own boat is a blessing. But if that comfort is to last, the confession must be followed by another commitment—the commitment to trust someone else who can.

Trusting the One Who Leads

Having reminded us of our inability to keep God's law or be our own leader, Paul continues his discourse in Romans 8 by outlining how we allow God to take the lead in our lives.

> *The mind of sinful man is death, but the mind controlled by the Spirit is life and peace; the sinful mind is hostile to God. It does not submit to God's law, nor can it do so. Those controlled by the sinful nature cannot please God. You, however, are controlled not by the sinful nature but by the Spirit, if the Spirit of God lives in you.* (Romans 8:6–9)

Do you notice the words Paul used to describe the Spirit's work in our hearts? *"The mind controlled by the Spirit."* In fairness to the apostle, we need to note that the actual word for control is not in this passage, but the translators of the New International Version chose that word to get across the concept intended by the two Greek words *kata pneuma*. This literally means "down into the spirit." It carries with it the notion of possession and ownership, as when one settles into a home or takes possession of a piece of property. With this in mind, consider what Paul is suggesting about the Spirit. We are to let him take full possession of our body. He is to be given complete control. If that thought is a bit unnerving and strange, join the club. Most humans don't like giving up control to anyone or anything.

Just think about the last time someone tried to drive your car . . . from the passenger seat. My wife is the one who gives me that experience most often. We'll be cruising home from dinner with friends and she'll say, "That light is yellow" or, "You need to turn right up here." She's not trying to be irritating, mind you. It's just that when we're driving in familiar territory, she sort of goes on autopilot. She corrects me without even thinking about it. And you can guess the results after a few minutes of spousal driver-training: "Would you like to drive?" I ask. "I'll pull over right here, and you can take the wheel."

"Oh, no, you drive. You're doing fine. I'll keep quiet."

And you know, I think she really means it. But habits are hard to break, and soon enough, I'm offering her the wheel again. Sound aggravating? Then consider how the Spirit must feel when we do the same thing to him. When we turn our lives over to Christ, we accept him as Lord. He is the leader, and we are the followers. But cruising down the path of life, I spot a shortcut that would avoid what appears to be unneeded pain or frustration. "Why don't we take a left here, Jesus. I think it might be an easier drive that way." Or maybe I grow impatient with the pace and start chiding him, "You know, we don't have to go quite this slowly. I'm sure it would be okay to speed through this stretch . . . cops hardly ever patrol around here!"

How long will it be before he turns to me and says, "Do you want to drive, or do you want me to?" It comes down to a matter of trust. Do I truly believe that the Spirit of God is capable of leading me where I need to go? This is not some thinly veiled fatalism. It is trusting God's sovereignty to manage all the twists and turns of life that are outside my control or even my awareness. Paul not only claims that God is capable of leading us, but questions our relationship if we don't allow him to do so, *"because those who are led by the Spirit of God are sons of God"* (Romans 8:14). One responsibility of sonship is trusting his fathership; giving up control demands that we decide once and for all who is going to drive. Thereafter, each day we hand him the wheel and trust his leading. When he veers off our "To Do" list or swerves away from our carefully planned schedule, we must determine not to pout or gripe but to

✦

How long will it be before Jesus turns to me and says, "Do you want to drive, or do you want me to?"

✦

trust his hand. Whether it's a late plane or a rained-out hunting trip, we trust his steering. After all, he knows much more than we about what tomorrow will bring and, therefore, what today should be.

Give the Leader Credit

> *Therefore, brothers, we have an obligation—but it is not to the sinful nature, to live according to it. For if you live according to the sinful nature, you will die; but if by the Spirit you put to death the misdeeds of the body, you will live.* (Romans 8:12–13)

Having put the steering wheel and our trust firmly in the Father's hand, good things will happen. Old habits will be conquered and new challenges will be met. Opportunities will knock, and doors will open. The danger, then, is that these victories and blessings will cause us, like Israel of old, to start taking credit for all these good things. Rather than praising the Spirit, we might begin to claim the credit for God's good driving.

Remember when the Israelites had finally fought their way back to the Red Sea to try a second time to cross into the Promised Land? Moses was preparing them for the battle of their lives, when two tribes, Reuben and Gad, sent representatives to him with a surprising question: "Can we stay on this side of the river?" Knowing that a mild temper was not one of the gifts God had given Moses, I wouldn't have dared suggest this to him from within ten feet. How could it be that after forty years of struggling, these two tribes wanted to skip entering into the Promised Land? What could have so undermined their determination to do God's will? A clue can be found in the preface to their request. "*The Reubenites and Gadites, who had very large herds and flocks, saw that the lands of Jazer and Gilead were suitable for livestock*" (Numbers 32:1).

They had acquired quite a bit during their wanderings, and rather than see these blessings as reasons to keep letting God drive, they saw them as reasons to take back the wheel. It seems they may not have been giving credit where credit was due. The results could have been catastrophic. Moses warned them that their lack of commitment could influence all Israel to give up the Promised Land, and he compared them to their forefathers as a *"brood of sinners, standing in the place of your fathers and making the Lord even more angry with Israel."* Thankfully for all concerned, the two stubborn tribes decided to leave the driving to God and joined in the victorious forces that took the Promised Land.

But our stories don't always end as happily as this one. While sometimes we threaten to take away the wheel, at other times we simply ignore the importance of giving thanks to the source of our blessings. By taking the honor ourselves, we rob God of the praise that is due him and deny the very reality of the Spirit's work. When we allow others to send the accolades our way, the witness that could bring praise to the power of God is denied:

"Yes, thank you; I did work awfully hard to make everything come out right."

"Yes, that was a brilliant decision I made."

"Yes, I pulled that one out of the fire at the last moment."

I realize that giving credit to God for decisions we make and events we are involved with can lead us into some dangerous waters. It's easy to stray into the marshy waters of hyper-spiritualism and start seeing the hand of God in the fact that the soda machine is out of Dr. Pepper. Further, it can prompt us to claim divine authority for our own choices, saying, "It must be right, for God has led me to do it." But a healthy diet of God's Word can balance any wild notions of personal infallibility. Moreover, these excesses are no less frightening than the opposite extreme—giving God no credit at all! Even our speech indicates that most of us are far closer to that end of the spectrum than the other.

In the late '70s a simple slogan became an evangelistic rage: "*I Found It!*" Whether on bumper stickers or buttons, it seemed every believer was proclaiming his faith with this little motto. I'm sure it helped some get into gospel-sharing conversations with nonbelievers, but the unintended residue of that line still lingers. Look closely at it. "I Found It!" Who's the subject of the sentence? Who claims credit for the work? Who's triumph is lauded there? The gospel leaves little room for this kind of bragging: *"For it is by grace you have been saved, through faith—and this not from yourselves, it is the gift of God"* (Ephesians 2:8). No "I Found It" in that sentence. In fact, we see just the opposite. God found us and presented us with the gift of salvation. We didn't hack our way through the jungle like some spiritual Indiana Jones. He lovingly brought Jesus to each of us through family and friends, Scripture and circumstance, till we could do little other than say, "Thank you, Lord, I accept your gift."

✦

> It would be the ultimate arrogance to say that I found the gospel. On the contrary; it was shoved down my throat.

✦

I know that for me, it would be the ultimate arrogance to say that I found the gospel. On the contrary; it was shoved down my throat by a loving mother and father while I protested almost every step of the way! No, my bumper sticker needs to read, "He Found Me!"

And please, don't stop there. Not only did he give us salvation, but every good gift we have comes from him. So why is it we don't give him more credit? Maybe it is because we are so unused to thinking in this way that we don't even notice God at work. It's hard to give him credit when we don't even spot what he's doing. But that may just mean we need a little practice.

For a long time, I would put my two oldest boys to bed the same way: I chased them. The game was completely predictable. At bed time, I'd look at the clock and growl, "I'm gonna chase two boys to their room; and if I catch them, I'll tickle them to death!" Off they would fly in a cloud of laughter down the hall and into their room with Dad in hot pursuit . . . slow, hot pursuit that is. I wanted to give them time to hide. Now this wasn't a real game of "find the boys," because they always hid in the exact same spot—their beds. But, nonetheless, the routine called for me to come into the bedroom and say, "Where are those boys? In the closet? No . . . Behind the door? No. Wait a minute . . ." By this time, I could see the covers quivering as they tried to stifle their giggles. "I think . . ." More giggles. "I think I see a boy in there!" And the covers would erupt in uncontrolled laughter.

Could you practice that with God? The next time something good happens to you, the next time an unplanned event interrupts your schedule or changes your itinerary, maybe you could say, "I think I see God in that!" And as you do, trusting his lead, you may find yourself beginning to dance with him.

Rejoice *in the Lord always. I will say it again: Rejoice! Let your gentleness be evident to all. The Lord is near. Do not be anxious about anything, but in everything, by prayer and petition, with thanksgiving, present your requests to God. And the peace of God, which transcends all understanding, will guard your hearts and your minds in Christ Jesus.*

✦ Philippians 4:4–7

Committing Your Soul to Celebration

STEP FOUR:
Choosing to Rejoice

It must have been an eerie sound that echoed off the stone walls and wafted through the midnight air. At first, one might have mistaken it for a moan or even an animal's wail—maybe one of the cows was out of its pen or a sheep had strayed from the fold. But if you listened closely, you could make out words . . . and notes. There was something almost . . . musical about it. It was a song!

But coming from a prison cell?

I don't know who first introduced me to the marvelous incongruities in the sixteenth chapter of Acts, but the scene has become a favorite. Within it, we discover the next step in learning to dance with God: using our God-given capacity for choosing to dance in spite of our difficulties. Before we can step onto the floor, we must learn how to make that choice. Sadly, many don't believe they have a choice. They feel trapped by their circumstances and life situations. They allow past hurts or present problems to limit their options. In short, they don't know that they can decide to dance and sing anyway. But Paul and Silas show us that they can.

To appreciate their song, we must first walk through the events that led up to the moonlight serenade in a Philippian jail. Luke tells the story in first person, and we pick up his account in Acts 16:16–18.

> *Once when we were going to the place of prayer, we were met by a slave girl who had a spirit by which she predicted the future. She earned a great deal of money for her owners by fortune-telling. This girl followed Paul and the rest of us, shouting, "These men are servants of the Most High God, who are telling you the way to be saved." She kept this up for many days. Finally Paul became so troubled that he turned around and said to the spirit, "In the name of Jesus Christ I command you to come out of her!" At that moment the spirit left her.*

Now, I've been heckled a bit while preaching and even had the odd comment tossed out from the audience during a particularly pointed sermon, but I have never experienced anything close to the kind of harassment that Paul and Silas faced. Their missionary tour had been rolling along quite well. Lydia and several others had responded to Christ, and the church was being planted in Europe. But then Satan stepped in. If he couldn't *stop* this evangelistic dynamic-duo, he would at least *distract* them with this crazed prophetess.

Did you notice that she followed them for *days?* Think about it. Every morning they'd get up and set off to the market square to meet people and preach a bit. Who would be waiting just outside the tent? "Good morning, boys!" She would holler and yell all the way into town, *"These men are servants of the most High God!"* So much for trying to keep a low profile. I'm sure it wore on their nerves, but what were they to do?

Maybe they tried the same tactic your mother suggested when you were teased at school—"Just ignore them, and they'll go away." But two days later and the crazy lady was still there—so much for Mom's great advice. Maybe Silas tried to reason with her and convince her that everyone had heard her announcement by now and she could take the rest of the day off. No soap. She wasn't leaving their side. Finally, Paul had to draw the line. Wheeling on her, he addressed the demon he knew to be the root of the problem. Through Christ's power it left the woman, and, we assume, she left Paul and Silas. But the peace was short-lived: *"When the owners of the slave girl realized that their hope of making money was gone, they seized Paul and Silas and dragged them into the marketplace to face the authorities."*

Now the owners got involved. Where these guys were while their slave was following Paul and Silas around all day, we don't know. But when she came home looking somewhat less *bedeviled,* they hit the ceiling. Who's going to want to hear prophecy from an ex-demon-possessed woman? This was not just an annoyance— we're talking loss of income, here. So armed with all they needed for a suit alleging economic hardship, they grabbed Paul and Silas and dragged them into the marketplace.

The wording in the text indicates that our two friends weren't keen on going downtown with this crew. You see, the marketplace was not only the shopping center of Philippi, it was the small claims court as well. Anybody with a gripe could air it there before a local tribunal and get swift, if not impartial, justice—and all that with an audience. In a day and age before cable TV, there were plenty of folks just hanging out at the marketplace waiting for something to happen.

With a broad accusation that could cover anything from inciting treason to cheating on taxes, the slave owners stirred up the crowd. *" 'These men are Jews, and are throwing our city into an uproar*

55

by advocating customs unlawful for us Romans to accept or practice.' The crowd joined in the attack against Paul and Silas."

Do you hear them play the prejudice card—*"These men are Jews!"* and the patriotic card—*"customs unlawful for us Romans!"* This is a no-holds-barred fight, and the crowd eagerly *"joined in the attack."* Ever been attacked by a crowd? Anyone who has watched footage of the LA riots won't take that phrase lightly. Our guys were in deep trouble. But just when things looked bleak, the magistrates showed up: Thank goodness, the sheriff is here! Now we'll get some order in the courtroom. Or will we?

> *And the magistrates ordered them to be stripped and beaten. After they had been severely flogged, they were thrown into prison, and the jailer was commanded to guard them carefully. Upon receiving such orders, he put them in the inner cell and fastened their feet in the stocks. (Acts 16:22–24)*

Okay. Who paid off the magistrates? They only stopped the attack long enough to strip and beat the victims! And this was no ordinary lashing. The word used here is *"flogged,"* and it deserves some attention.

Several years ago I stood in a museum looking at a little table encased in glass. It wasn't remarkable, really. Made of wood and standing about three feet tall, it looked like someone's well-worn breakfast table. What prompted its inclusion in the museum was its function: it had been the flogging table for the Nazi concentration camp at Dachau. A small placard explained how prisoners were bent over this little table with their feet and hands lashed to the legs. A long stick or metal rod was used to beat their backs until the flesh was raw.

Paul and Silas were probably flogged with a cat-o'-nine-tails—a favorite tool of the Romans. It was made of leather and, as the name suggests, had nine strands coming from the handle. In the end of each strand a knot was tied, often around a bit of stone or bone to add just a little more bite to the lashing. From this instrument of torture, the missionaries took between twenty and forty lashes.

Needless to say, Paul and Silas were in no condition to dance when they were finally taken to the jail. And once there, the jailer made sure they couldn't move, much less dance, by tying them to a post or stone in the middle of the cell. This process, often indicated by the phrase *"placing them in the inner cell,"* meant that their hands were not even free to tend to the wounds on their backs.

So there they sat—on the cold, damp, stone floor of a Roman jail.

They had been harassed, grabbed, publicly accused, attacked, beaten, flogged, and bound—and all in the same day! Makes you stop and think about the times you've griped, "Man, I've had a rough day!"

And how did they end this perfect day? You take the quiz:

If I were in their spot, I would have . . .
>   a. cried myself to sleep.
>   b. whined, complained, and said it wasn't fair.
>   c. declared my innocence and demanded my captors grant me an appeal.
>   d. called on God to avenge me on my accusers and their children's children.
>   e. sung all three verses of "There Is Sunshine in My Soul Today!"

Time's up. Were you honest? Looking at the whole picture, the choice made by Paul and Silas is nothing less than stunning. It also makes the later response of the jailer more understandable. He, too, must have been dumbfounded at the resilience of these two, beat-up Jews—and rightly so. They had exercised one of the greatest abilities the creator has afforded us: they had chosen to rejoice and dance with God despite their surroundings.

✦ The Choice to Rejoice

Let me be clear. This is more than making lemonade when life gives you lemons. It is the capacity to dance when you can barely crawl. It is the choice to sing when you feel like crying. And it is doing so not out of ignorance or blind faith but because of an awareness of God's sovereignty and your confidence in him. Paul himself gives us an insight into this when he writes back to the congregation that was born during his tumultuous visit. Knowing what he experienced in Philippi, his words take on new meaning.

> *Rejoice in the Lord always. I will say it again: Rejoice! Let your gentleness be evident to all. The Lord is near. Do not be anxious about anything, but in everything, by prayer and petition, with thanksgiving, present your requests to God. And the peace of God, which transcends all understanding, will guard your hearts and your minds in Christ Jesus. Finally, brothers, whatever is true, whatever is noble, whatever is right, whatever is pure, whatever is lovely, whatever is admirable—if anything is excellent or praiseworthy— think about such things.* (Philippians 4:4–8)

In this passage Paul presents three simple instructions; if we follow them, we, too, will be able to sing in a prison cell or dance in our darkest hour.

#1: Rejoice

He begins with a command: *"Rejoice in the Lord."* This is not a suggestion or a request. And lest we mistake his intent, he repeats it. "Are you hearing me?" he is asking. Why so forceful, Paul?

Could it be that Paul knew there would be those who would jump ship right here. They would claim that it just wasn't their style to rejoice or maybe that it felt awkward or inconvenient. You know the kind of person I'm talking about—one of those perennially dour folks who can brighten up a room by leaving it. Some seem to have trained black clouds to behave like Mary's little lamb and follow them wherever they go. When you ask them how things are going, you had better brace yourself for a litany of woes. "My job! My son! My back!" Take your pick—they can gripe profusely about any of them. And don't get into a session of "I can top that" with them. If you've got a toothache, they just had four root canals. If your dog was hit by a car, theirs was mauled to death by a wild lion on their own front lawn.

Now, it's only fair to note that all of us have a bit of the griper in us. Surveys have shown that most people will repeat a bit of tragic news eight to one over a piece of good news. I suppose we find a perverse comfort in hearing the misfortunes of others. But the chronic cases are of a different breed. They aren't just amateur sticks-in-the-mud: these guys are pros. As a friend of mine loves to say, "They are such stinkers that if you put Odor-Eaters in their shoes, they would disappear altogether." These individuals must be called to face up to the command of the Lord as written by Paul. It is their duty to quit being so grumpy! Whether they like it or not, they had better start rejoicing.

✦

Choosing to rejoice is more than making lemonade when life gives you lemons—it is the capacity to dance when you can barely crawl.

✦

If you detect a note of harshness here, you're right. I admit to having a hard time feeling sorry for this lot. They cause others such misery with their negative attitudes. Some have actually driven off young believers from the faith with their sour spirits. But I am also harsh because this is not my particular problem. I'm typically a pretty positive person, thank God, so it's easy for me to be stern about something I don't have a problem with. It's like the old definition of the difference between major and minor surgery—if *you* have it, it's minor; if *I* have it, it's major.

#2: Ask God for Help

So how do cynical saints change their stripes? I don't want to resort to telling them that "The beatings will continue until morale improves!" Christian joy cannot be forced or coerced. It is a gift from God, and as such, any who want it must begin by asking for it. Listen to Paul's advice: *"Do not be anxious about anything, but in everything, by prayer and petition, with thanksgiving, present your requests to God."*

After commanding rejoicing Paul says, "Don't let your problems control your attitude. Ask God for help!" If you want to replace the bitterness or negativity you have fallen into with rejoicing, request that of God. It may sound offhanded, but if more of us prayed each morning, "God give me a joyous and positive attitude today," the world would be a much more enjoyable place to inhabit. It may be that if you've been a grump for years, the words of James are aimed at you: *"You have not for you ask not."*

#3: Focus on the Positive

Next, Paul gives us some practical advice on choosing to rejoice. He suggests that the heart of the problem . . . is your heart . . . and making sure it is focused on the right things. While God will *"guard your heart and your mind,"* it is you who must focus them on what Paul defines as the true, noble, right, pure, and lovely. Doesn't leave us much room for meditating on past injustices or present irritations, does he? His decree is that the Christian mind should be filled with good stuff. And what's inside will come out, in our words as well as our deeds.

Practical ways to tackle this task are many. My favorite is one I believe originated with Ben Franklin, but a friend of mine, Marvin Phillips, added a twist I've adopted. Franklin, the revolutionary American philosopher and statesman, recommended that decisions be made by drawing up a list of pros and cons on a sheet of paper—pros on the right and cons on the left. When the list is complete, you can quickly scan the results and identify the best choice. Now, instead of making a list of pros or cons, take a sheet and list your blessings and gripes. Put all the things that make you want to sing praises on the left-hand column and the ones that make you frown on the right—you know you're in trouble if you need a second sheet of paper for the list on the right.

Got that done? Now, a view of life without God might mean that you just add up the pluses and take away the minuses. If you end up with a positive number, count yourself lucky. But that's not what Paul prescribes. Instead, tear your paper in half, separating the two lists. What you should now have is a list of blessings in one hand and a list of problems in the other. Fold up the list of problems and put it away. Don't worry. You won't forget anything on that list easily. As Tevye says in *Fiddler on the Roof*, "Good news comes and goes, but bad news is here to stay." Now take the list of blessings and look it over. Memorize it. Meditate on it. Recite it to yourself. Give thanks for it. Talk about it with your friends. Soon you will actually be *"thinking on these things"* without conscious effort.

> ✦
>
> There's a whole lot more to changing your behavior than just having the right information.
>
> ✦

If this sounds a bit Pollyannish, I dare you to try it. Remember, this concept comes not from pop psychology but from a fellow who spent the night singing in prison after a day in hell. As you begin seeing life in a different way, you may even shock yourself and start dancing the divine dance of joy.

✦ Four to Get You Started

Now a word for the hard-nosed cynics: if you're staring at a blank sheet of blessings, you may need a jump start. So let me share my list of blessings with you—it's simple and easy to remember.

A Father Who Will Never Leave Me

There's no one like my heavenly Father, and there's no one who can make him stop loving me. Our relationship is intimate and firm. He has adopted me so that I can address him as a son, not as a slave. *"For you did not receive a spirit that makes you a slave again to fear, but you received the Spirit of sonship. And by him we cry, 'Abba, Father'"* (Romans 8:14–15).

Just watch a little child run to his father when he's frightened or hurt. When those big arms wrap around that little body, there's nothing that can penetrate that peace. So it is with my Lord. Whenever I'm in need, he is available, and I'll never be too old to crawl up into his lap. As a child, I could stand anything if my dad was by my side; and as an adult, I don't have to give up that comforting feeling. With my heavenly Father near, I'm always ready to dance.

Forgiveness for All My Sins

Whether big or small, God has wiped them all away. And he doesn't keep them in a drawer so he can beat me with them whenever I come calling. Listen to the prophet's words:

> *Who is a God like you,*
> *who pardons sin and forgives the transgression*
> *of the remnant of his inheritance?*
> *You do not stay angry forever*
> *but delight to show mercy.*
>
> *You will again have compassion on us;*
> *you will tread our sins underfoot*
> *and hurl all our iniquities into the depths of the sea.*
> (Micah 7:18–19)

How far away would you like to put your sins? You can run from them, lie about them, try to pay for them, but it just won't work. Only God can remove your sins: *"As far as the east is from the west, so far has he removed our transgressions from us"* (Psalm 103:12). And the good news is—all I have to do is ask. "Father, forgive me" may be the most powerful words a human can utter. They can free your soul of the burden that keeps you from dancing.

A Family That Can't Get Rid of Me

God did not send Jesus to establish a corporation. He sent him to redeem a family. I am connected by the blood of Christ to all who have placed their faith in him. Whether or not they like me or agree with me, we are family by God's decree. *"Both the one who makes men holy and those who are made holy are of the same family. So Jesus is not ashamed to call them brothers"* (Hebrews 2:11).

If God has brought me into this wonderful, worldwide family, then no one else can kick me out. If I choose to remove myself through willful choice, I have that power. But as long as the blood of Christ covers me, I am a child of the king and an heir to the throne. Now that's worth dancing about!

A Future That Can't Be Taken Away from Me

Death stands at the end of the trail, waiting like a greedy creditor to collect all we have. No U-Haul behind a hearse can get past him. You leave like you came—with nothing. But even that grim-faced reaper can't take my future away. Jesus assures me of that: *"In my Father's house are many rooms; if it were not so, I would have told you. I am going there to prepare a place for you. And if I go and prepare a place for you, I will come back and take you to be with me that you also may be where I am"* (John 14:1–3).

We'll save some thoughts on this topic for the chapter on facing death, but let me at least include this here: Ask a young girl what she's going to do with her future, and you'll get a long list of exciting possibilities. Ask an eighty-year-old, and he might slap your face for being impertinent. The future isn't something older people like to dwell on. As a senior citizen friend of mine says, "At my age, I don't even buy green bananas!" But the Christian has a future that can't be robbed by cancer, AIDS, or nuclear war—it is locked up tight within the promise of God. Because of that, I look forward to an eternity of dancing with him.

Well, there's my short list. Four simple things that I have written on a post-it note in my heart. This list reminds me that I can choose what I dwell on, that I can focus my thoughts on the good and noble things in my life rather than the gripes and complaints, and that I can dance despite my surroundings.

So what about you? Can you make your own list? Reflect on the good things God has put in your life. Don't overlook past experiences and precious memories. Consider faithful friends and loving family. And when your list is done, don't hide it in a drawer; keep it handy for emergencies. Post it on your bathroom mirror. Tack it on your dashboard. You never know when the crowd may attack or the day may go sour.

Then make a commitment. Take a solemn vow that you will dance with God even when you don't feel like it. Not because you must, but because you have so much to dance about. Take the celebration pledge: I will rejoice in my Lord every day! It can make a world of difference in you, and it won't go unnoticed.

Eunice Brown, a dear Christian friend, suffered for weeks in the final stages of pancreatic cancer. The pain was immense, yet despite her agony, her prayers and thoughts seemed always to focus on the blessings God had given her. I commented to her husband about her continued positive spirit and wondered aloud how she did it. He quietly took me to her bathroom and pointed to a scrap of paper stuck in the corner of her dressing mirror. In her own handwriting it said, "This is the day that the Lord has made. I *will* rejoice and be glad in it!"

Though outwardly we are wasting away, yet inwardly we are being renewed day by day. For our light and momentary troubles are achieving for us an eternal glory that far outweighs them all. So we fix our eyes not on what is seen, but on what is unseen. For what is seen is temporary, but what is unseen is eternal.

✦ 2 Corinthians 4:16–18

Dancing
on Thin Air

STEP FIVE:
Seeing the Invisible

It happened again. I was making a quick shopping trip to the local mall when I got sidetracked by one of those 3-D picture displays. They are hard to miss, as there's always a crowd of frustrated people gathered around staring intently at these apparently unintelligible splashes of color. If you look at them long enough in just the right way, they will trick your eyes into seeing a third dimension within them . . . or so the guy who sells them assures you. Problem is, most folks can't see it at will. Sometimes you can, and sometimes you can't. And just about the time you decide to give up trying, the guy next to you shouts, "I see it!" Who knows; when they collect all the goofy fads of the '90s for an exhibit at the Smithsonian, they may dedicate a whole room to these "works of art."

Interestingly enough, I have some friends who feel that faith in God is just as illusive as the hidden 3-D picture—they have such a hard time seeing him. They are like the famous cosmonaut who looked outside his space capsule window and proclaimed that there is no God. Yet the apostle Paul claims that it is impossible to look anywhere without seeing him. How can these two viewpoints be so different? Believers discover that an indispensable part of dancing with God is learning to see the unseen dance floor.

Consider the famous scene from one of Steven Spielberg's Indiana Jones film. I'm an "Indy" fan, I confess. Those movies never fail to give me a thrill, no matter how many times I watch them. One of my favorite moments is from the last film in the trilogy that recounts the professor's attempt to find and retrieve the Holy Grail—the cup that Christ drank from at the Last Supper. Legends say that this cup would give immortality to anyone who drank from it, so naturally it was kept in a mystic cave behind numerous booby traps.

Indiana Jones manages to get past every barrier, only to be faced with a final, apparently insurmountable one—a huge canyon stands between him and the room where the cup is kept. To cross it, he must take a "leap of faith" over a chasm hundreds of feet wide. If you've never seen the film, I hate to spoil a great moment, but when Indy finally swallows his fear, closes his eyes, and takes the first step in faith, a previously invisible walkway materializes beneath his feet. He walks without difficulty over what had appeared to be thin air to retrieve the cup and bring the film to its climax.

The image of walking on thin air well introduces our final step in learning to dance with God. The believer is called to dance with the Maker on an unseen dance floor, responding to invisible realities and keeping time with inaudible music. Sound complex? It's just what Paul told the Corinthians to do in his second letter to that troubled church.

Therefore we do not lose heart. Though outwardly we are wasting away, yet inwardly we are being renewed day by day. For our light and momentary troubles are achieving for us an eternal glory that far outweighs them all. So we fix our eyes not on what is seen, but on what is unseen. For what is seen is temporary, but what is unseen is eternal. (2 Corinthians 4:16–18)

The apostle begins with an ugly truth: life takes its toll on all of us. The day-to-day challenges of living in a world that is slowly crumbling and bodies that are quickly aging can cause the best of us to lose heart and quit dancing. After all, how can we look in the mirror week after week and watch our hairlines making a beeline for our behinds and not get frustrated?

Paul addresses this reality with candor. "Yes," he replies, "we are wasting away outwardly." But just about the time we're ready to put on the cynic's sandwich board sign, "We're All Gonna Die, So Give Up!" the apostle lets us in on a secret. He points to the invisible realities around us and offers glasses through which we can see the unseen dance floor. In language nothing short of commanding, he says, "Fix your eyes on what is unseen." It's an odd statement at best. He is literally saying, "Look at what you cannot look at, not at what you can." Learning this one "dance step" may be the most important skill any believer can develop. Without it, we are trapped in the depressing here-and-now world, with only fleeting victories and temporary achievements. With it, we open our spiritual eyes to the real world of God's power and promises.

But how do you develop the ability to see this marvelous unseen world? You can begin by taking the glasses Paul offers and trying them on. They will allow you to see only that which is of eternal importance. Imagine putting them on and seeing . . . nothing. Do you notice what you can't see? The first half of Paul's important premise spells it out.

✦ What Is Seen Is Temporary

"What is seen is temporary." What an earthshaking reality! Everything we can see with our human eyes is temporary and thus of limited eternal value. From the houses we break our backs to buy to the clothing we take such pains to select, the Bible teaches us that every bit of our visible universe is temporary. It's no more permanent than a throw-away camera or the wrapper on a candy bar. Christ challenged the disciples' thinking with this fact as he left the temple grounds for the last time before his crucifixion.

As they walked out of the temple, the disciples noted, as many had before them, the sheer size of the stones that composed the great structure's walls. Indeed, archeologists tell us that some of these stones weighed over two tons. The permanence and stability of that massive building must have been overwhelming. Yet, as they marveled at it, Jesus told them that this centerpiece of Israel's history and monument to her endurance would be completely destroyed. *"Not one stone here will be left on another; every one will be thrown down"* (Mark 13:2). Unthinkable! The temple? Temporary? Their reaction sounds like that of a child when she first learns that Mom and Dad won't live forever. "It can't be! When will this occur?"

As with most of us, they missed the point. It is not the *when*, but the *what* of that prophecy that mattered. The date of the temple's destruction some forty years later or the name of the Roman conqueror who would accomplish it was less important than the fact that it would be destroyed. They could not imagine life without the temple, just as we cannot imagine life without America or our city or our homes. Yet all of these are just as temporary as Jerusalem's temple.

This unpleasant but essential fact must be embraced and affirmed if we are to dance with God. Because he decreed that all the things we see around us will be destroyed in the final fire, we cannot allow ourselves to become controlled by them. We must touch and hold them without grasping and clinging to them. We

70

must treat them with respect without imbuing them with eternal value. The rule of thumb must become: *If you can touch it with your hands and see it with your eyes, it can't be that important.* We know that the treasures we guarded so jealously as kids, from baseball card collections to stuffed animal menageries, quickly became the stuffing for our own basements and attic trunks. As adults, we learn that the technological prize of January is quickly replaced by the faster, better contraption of June. (When's the last time you tried to sell an old computer? They go from priceless dream machines to worthless boat anchors with lightening speed!) Yet, we spend countless dollars and hours acquiring, maintaining, and updating our collections of treasures and trophies. We become trapped in the endless cycle of trying to satisfy an appetite for possessions that always demands just one more.

Keep in mind that Paul doesn't say possessions are evil—just *temporary*. And in that word lies the key. There is such a difference in the way we treat something we believe will be long lasting as opposed to that which we recognize is expendable. And when it becomes clear that an item is temporary and of little future use, its value changes accordingly. A recent garage sale helped remind me of this point.

◆

If you can touch it with your hands and see it with your eyes, it can't be that important.

◆

Cathryn had decided to clear the clutter in our closets with a yard sale. I'm the type who never throws anything away, so there was plenty of fodder for her little enterprise. I wasn't excited about the whole thing, but she didn't demand my help; in fact, she seemed glad to tackle the project on her own. I soon saw why. After covering the lawn with the kids' old toys and some of her old shoes, she opened our garage door and used the tension bar as a hanger. Before I knew it, she had half the contents of my closet hanging out for sale! Several of my older suits and sport jackets were displayed for the neighbors to pick through. And if seeing my favorite old clothes being offered to strangers wasn't bad enough, I felt downright insulted when she started putting price tags on them! "You can't sell that suit for five dollars!" I protested.

"We'll see," she said. "I can always lower it to two-fifty if nobody bites at first."

"No, no. I mean that's too cheap. That was one of my favorite suits. I wore it all the time. You can't sell it!"

"Okay. Put it on," she said, holding it out to me. In my indignation, I took the bait without thinking about how long it had been since I had worn that jacket. I couldn't even get it buttoned.

"This thing has shrunk," I mumbled. She smiled and put a $2.50 price tag on it.

As I watched the sale progress, I was struck by how easily we become attached to junk that doesn't really matter. It's a real challenge to avoid overestimating the worth of the stuff that clutters our life. But consider the fights that could be avoided and the relationships that could be saved if we could get the right perspective on possessions. No wonder James declares that the source of fights and quarrels among us is the *"desires that battle within you. You want something but don't get it."* How many of the things that we want are in the visible realm? And how often do the unseen values of relationships or inner values like integrity and love get sacrificed on the altar of the seen? Paul's command can bring so much freedom: *"Fix your eyes not on what is seen, but on what is unseen."*

My father was my greatest teacher when it came to putting this truth into practice. For years our family car was a blue, Ford station wagon. We bought it brand new from the showroom floor. Its two-toned design was sleek and smooth . . . for a station wagon, anyway. And it had the latest gadgetry—push-button transmission and windows that actually rolled themselves up and down. And to top it all, my sister and brother and I had two whole seats to ourselves, one of which actually faced backwards! From the moment we rode in it, we loved it.

The first time we brought it home, Dad parked it in front of our house, which was next door to the church. But as he got out, he did an odd thing—he put the ignition key on top of the visor above the driver's side and left the driver's door unlocked. My mother began immediately with what I later learned was an ongoing protest. "Now Jeff," she said, "you can't do that with *this* car. It's brand new!" It seems Dad had made a practice through the years of leaving the car unlocked and the key in that same spot. Mom contended that was a great idea if your goal was getting your car stolen. But Dad's reasoning was simple: "If I need to loan someone the car, the key will always be there." It was his way of putting in real terms a proper perspective on what we owned. Jesus' own directions in this matter back up his approach: *"Give to the one who asks you, and do not turn away from the one who wants to borrow from you"* (Matthew 5:42).

That kind of generosity is only possible when the value of one's possessions is never rated above the value of one's friends. While I confess that I haven't followed my father's example with my car keys, the principle he taught did sink in. I am confident that I am far more generous because of his modeling. Oh sure, I've lost my share of books or tools through the years because I was willing to loan them to just about anybody. And on occasion someone who borrowed my car wasn't very careful about keeping oil in the crankcase, but I've gained so much more than I've ever lost through the blessings that come from generosity. And I've profited more than words can say from knowing that things we can see just aren't that important.

But you don't have to have a father who keeps his keys on the visor to demonstrate that truth. One family I know wrote down their "core values" and displayed them on their refrigerator door. One of them read: "People are always more valuable than things." I certainly agree with that statement, but Paul would attach another clause to it: The invisible is always more important than the seen. Anyone who chooses to dance with God knows this instinctively, because the unseen universe contains the eternal treasures that will never fade or depreciate.

So now that we've pledged to keep our eyes off the seen world, what is in this unseen world that is so precious? Let Paul's words guide us again.

✦ Seeing the Unseen Realm

"What is unseen is eternal." The invisible realm is where God waits for us. He chose, since the outset, to be the God of the unseen. *Jehovah Olam*, one of the Hebrew names for God used in the Old Testament, can be translated "the God of Mystery" or "the God of the Unseen Realm." He revealed his mysterious nature in thunder, fire, and smoke to the patriarchs, and in sandals and a toga to the apostles. But today he can only be seen in the unseen. To see God we must look with eyes of faith past the world around us and see the invisible Almighty. And when our eyes focus so that we can see him, what else do we see that is eternal? The Scriptures suggest at least three important things.

The Love of God

Psalm 136 is easily the most repetitive song in the collection of Hebrew hymns we call the Psalms. In it the writer has a favorite line that he repeats some twenty-six times. Like the "hook" of a pop song, it is the phrase he wants us to remember. Historians suggest that the psalm was probably constructed as an antiphonal hymn. The leader would sing the first half of each verse, and the congregation would sing the second half in response. And it is the second half that contains the repeated phrase, *"The love of the Lord endures forever."* Just imagine being a Hebrew child at the tribal worship. When the leader announced the singing of that psalm, you would brace yourself. "Here we go with twenty-six verses of the same thing—'The love of the Lord endures forever.'" How monotonous! But it must have gotten the message through. If you forgot every other line to this psalm, you wouldn't forget this truth—God's love is not a temporary thing. The mountains may pass away and the seas may dry up, but the Lord's invisible and unseen love is eternal!

We need that kind of strong reminder when we look at the temporary loves around us. Relationships let us down, and "best friends" move across the country and slowly fade into history. Truly dependable love is a rare commodity, and no one offers it like the Lord. He never, ever gives up on us. His secure and abiding love gives the believer a solid platform from which to function, an unshakable truth on which to stand: "My God cares for me. My God is committed to me. My God will not stop loving me." With that verity written on our hearts, we can step out in faith to dance through circumstances that appear as impassable as the Grand Canyon. We move not flippantly or carelessly but confidently, because of his great love for us. It is the affirmation that every human seeks. But no human relationship, however close and comforting, can bring the soul-securing strength that comes when you look full into the eternal love God has for us.

Unfortunately, many never focus on that invisible source of strength because of their misconceptions about God's feelings toward them. Years of browbeating from religious authorities have convinced them that God is more like a global policeman, just waiting for the opportunity to write them out a spiritual citation. With that image of God, no wonder many young people have little interest in prayer and even less in church. And it is equally not surprising that they would go looking for affirmation everywhere else—through gangs, drugs, sexual gratification, money, and power. But only God's love provides the affirmation that allows us to dance freely and joyously.

Knowing that his love is as invisible as it is timeless, maybe we should try the psalmist's approach in our own worship. We could just sit and sing over and over again, "Jesus loves me this I know" or "The steadfast love of the Lord never ceases" . . . or maybe we should just remind ourselves each morning that the first thing we can't see today is God and his eternal love.

75

The Words of Christ

Just as eternal as the love of God is the truth that Christ brought us; his words will have value forever. Jesus himself is called "the Word" by John in his gospel; and the writer makes clear that as the Word, he was a part of creation: *"Through him all things were made; without him nothing was made that has been made. In him was life, and that life was the light of men"* (John 1:3–4). In a society where words and information have become the true units of power, the words of Christ are among the best known in all of history. They have shaped the thinking of kings and have confounded the scholars who would seek to discredit them. And his words have changed lives all across the globe. From remote villages in the Australian outback to downtown Manhattan, followers of Jesus testify to the power of his teachings. The words of Christ stand as the most influential ever spoken.

"But wait," I hear you protest, "aren't the words of Christ visible? Can't we read them in the Bible?" Though the words of Jesus may be put in print, and in that sense be visible, the truth that is the Word can't be bound up in pages or scrolls. That's why God says through the prophet Jeremiah, *"I will put my laws in their minds and write them on their hearts. I will be their God, and they will be my people"* (Hebrews 8:10). Through the centuries, those who oppose the Bible have made the mistake of believing that they could destroy its truth by destroying its pages. Though the Bible has been both banned and burned through the centuries, the power it proclaims has not been diminished. Those truths and the words that convey them to us are destined to be important throughout eternity. Jesus himself guarantees their ability to withstand the winds of time: *"Heaven and earth will pass away, but my words will never pass away"* (Matthew 24:35).

Yet despite all their eternal power, the words of God aren't always the words that we treasure in our hearts. When's the last time you conscientiously worked at committing some portion of Scripture to memory? Memorizing Bible verses is almost a passé activity with modern Christians—like Sunday dinners on the grounds, it seems outdated. After all, when you can keep the entire Bible on your laptop computer and do phrase searches and cross references in the blink of an eye, why take the time to memorize it?

Unfortunately, the wonder of computer technology doesn't include instant recall when in crisis. I just can't imagine being in a conversation with a friend whose mother just passed away and saying, "You know, Jesus said something that would be very comforting to you right now, and if I can boot up my Toshiba, here, I'll try and find it!" There is no substitute for hiding the eternal words of Christ in your heart.

Moreover, the complex and wonderful brains that God gave us will feed on and store whatever information they are regularly exposed to, regardless of its relative importance. I am reminded of this by the folks who protest that they are unable to commit Jesus' words to memory. Well . . . let's try something. I'll start a sentence and you finish it:

> Mary had a little . . .
> Oh say can you see by the . . .
> You are my sunshine, my only . . .
> If you can't say something nice . . .
> Oh, beautiful for spacious skies for amber . . .

You get the point. When we hear something often enough, or when we feel something is useful or important, we'll commit it to memory. And aren't the words of Christ useful and important?

Dancing with God demands that we have his words ringing in the unseen halls of our hearts. They must set up a rhythm of their own in our thinking. While the seen world shouts that first place is best and that might makes right, the words of Christ whisper that the last shall be first and that the servant's place is the position of true greatness. If we store his words in our hearts, we'll find them springing to our lips just when we need them. As we listen to the silent drummer of his teachings, as we allow them to echo in our souls, our relationships and daily decisions will reflect his divine tempo. Hearing his soundless voice with the ears of our spirit, we gain the surety of the timeless truths he has revealed. Could that have been the writer's intent when he said *"let the words of Christ live in you richly!"*?

The Life of the Soul

Though invisible to the naked eye, God placed something at the core of our beings that is designed to last forever. The thing we call our soul is the spiritual component of our person. It is impervious to the maladies and problems of our bodies—it cannot contract cancer, develop arthritis, or get wrinkles. But it can be disabled and weakened through a lack of attention. While we wouldn't think of making our bodies go without food for a week, our souls can be impoverished and exhausted for lack of spiritual care. Moreover, if we want to participate in the dance of life with the creator of the universe, the welfare of our unseen spiritual side must be addressed.

If physical dancing can be an aerobic exercise, it's safe to say that dancing with God also takes plenty of inner fortitude. When no care is taken to support the soul and feed the spirit, don't expect to waltz through the ebb and flow of life without feeling constantly winded and exhausted. Though the soul is unseen, the effects of neglecting it are all too evident. Nagging depression, bitterness, and pessimism are just a few of the signs of a malnourished spirit. The health of one's soul may well be gauged by the tenor of one's life.

But herein lies the battle: making time to maintain one's physical body is challenging enough—even with the visible flab there to motivate you; but the discipline necessary to invest energy in caring for your invisible, eternal insides is even tougher. If only there were a spiritual "Solo-flex" machine that would firm and tone the contours of the soul like those fancy treadmills touted on cable TV sculpt the Jack Lalane look-alikes who demonstrate them. At least we can use their approach as a model for our invisible body building. Two techniques in particular can strengthen our souls—*sitting* and *stretching.*

Time spent sitting alone with God is the foundation of our spiritual health. No writer knew this better than the psalmist. He saw his own soul go from fit and trim to flabby and decrepit. He went from being God's hero, the boy who slew the giant, to Satan's pawn, the man who fell for Bathsheba—in just fourteen chapters. And what does he learn from all this?

> *As the deer pants for streams of water,*
> *so my soul pants for you, O God.*
> *My soul thirsts for God, for the living God.*
> *When can I go and meet with God?*
> (Psalm 42:1–2)

Listening to David, we hear a man who knows what his soul needs. He desires time with God like a thirsty deer craves water. And not just any time, but time *alone* with him. Too much of our thinking about communion with God is clouded by the importance of communion with Christians. While the latter is needed, the former is essential. In a world that constantly allows for human contact, whether by cellular phone, fax, or e-mail, getting alone with God becomes increasingly difficult. One busy executive I know simply told his secretary that when the small workroom door in his office was shut, she shouldn't even think about knocking. It was his special time to be sequestered with God. Jesus recommends a closet. Others have turned off the radio and unplugged the car-phone to make their commute a time of meditation and prayer. Find a time that works for you, and dedicate yourself to nurturing the unseen, inside man by sitting and listening, pondering and praising, alone with your Maker.

After you've learned to sit, then stretch!

Of the many ways that one might exercise the unseen man, I've become certain that the soul's muscles can best be worked out through extending service and love to others. Consider Christ's choice to associate with the needy and outcast. How easy it would have been to just "hang with the boys." He could have spent the entirety of his time with those who would fawn over his every word and supply his every need, but by his own definition, the Son of Man came to *"seek and serve."* He set an example for us by stretching the limits of his patience and generosity with those most in need. He extended the limits of love to take in both the harlot and hypocrite.

✦

The hidden reality of selfless service is that it is one of the few things of eternal value we can do with our finite time.

✦

So, how often do you give your spirit a good stretch? A high-cholesterol diet of immediate gratification and no-brainer conversation with only those who agree with me can leave me ill prepared to serve the hurting and lonely. They are seldom grateful in attitude and often inconvenient in timing. But it is here that my spirit gets its workout. And it is here that my soul gains the stamina to dance with the greatest Spirit of all. By reaching into my invisible resources and drawing out the strength to go a second mile or give an extra hour for someone who needs it, I strengthen the resolve that the Spirit gives to focus on that which is *unseen.* The hidden reality of selfless service is that it is one of the few things of eternal value we can do with our finite time.

So if your spiritual man is a bit peaked, maybe it's time for some sit and stretch exercising. It may hurt at first, but then again, if you want to dance with God for an eternity, your soul had best be conditioned for the long haul!

Overcoming a Handful of EXCUSES

✦ SECTION TWO
5 Diseases That Stop
the Music

"I'm too busy."
"I don't know how."
"I don't feel comfortable."
"I tried it once and failed."

When you don't want to do something, any old excuse will do. But excuses that are given often enough and passionately enough have a strange way of transforming. They can turn into life-altering diseases that plague our spirits and paralyze our wills. They become spiritual shackels that obscure our vision, leaving us incapable of walking, much less dancing.

But no disease can triumph over the Great Physician. When he lays the two-edged scalpel of his Word to our excuses, they melt away to reveal the fear or pride from which they came. And when he adds the laser light of his Spirit, even the paralyzed can be made whole again. Oh, this is no easy task. But then again, he is no common Lord.

So don't worry about filling out any forms, just sit down and open up your heart. The doctor is in.

Now there is in Jerusalem near the Sheep Gate a pool, which in Aramaic is called Bethesda and which is surrounded by five covered colonnades. Here a great number of disabled people used to lie—the blind, the lame, the paralyzed. One who was there had been an invalid for thirty-eight years. When Jesus saw him lying there and learned that he had been in this condition for a long time, he asked him, "Do you want to get well?"

"Sir," the invalid replied, "I have no one to help me into the pool when the water is stirred. While I am trying to get in, someone else goes down ahead of me."

Then Jesus said to him, "Get up! Pick up your mat and walk." At once the man was cured; he picked up his mat and walked.

✦ John 5:2–9

S • I • X

Bethesda Blight – The Coward's Paralysis

"Can't Dance, Don't Ask Me!"

I stood with my back hugging the wall at the only high school dance I ever attended. I was a senior, and thanks to my parents' strong convictions, I had never even seen a school dance before. When the flyers came around for the Senior Sock Hop, I just couldn't resist. There was no way I could talk them into letting me attend the prom, but I was able to finagle permission to just go and *watch* at this '50s-style party. I really had no intention of dancing, mind you, and my folks thought I was old enough to see for myself what the big "no-no" looked like in person.

So there I stood, sporting jeans with the cuffs turned up over white socks and loafers, hair carefully roached back, and a spotless white T-shirt. I imagined that I looked like Fonzie's nice younger brother. The music was loud and only vaguely familiar—I wasn't old enough to buy records when Buddy Holly was king—but the noise of the party and the excitement of being at my first dance were plenty to keep my adrenaline pumping quite nicely.

Then it happened. This cute girl from my French class spotted me and made a beeline for my corner. "Hey, what a shock to see you here! Wanna dance?" As odd as it may seem, I was completely unprepared for this question. Social customs being what they were, I had wrongly assumed that only boys asked girls to dance. I thought I could just meander around the hall watching everyone else without being put on the spot. But here I stood being asked to dance by a beautiful girl, and the only truthful answer was more embarrassing than I had imagined.

◆

I was being asked to dance by a beautiful girl, and the only truthful answer was more embarrassing than I had imagined.

◆

"I can't," I whispered.

She shook her head and said "What? I can't hear you."

Leaning closer, I said louder, "I can't!" She shook her head again, so I just hollered, "*I can't dance!*"

Somehow I managed to time that yell right during a moment of silence in whatever song the band was playing. At least twenty-five people in the immediate area turned to stare at us.

Ignoring the gawkers, she said, "Oh sure you can. Don't worry, just try." I smiled and mumbled something about, "Thanks, but no thanks," and managed to slip away from her and out of the building feeling a combination of stupidity and guilt. What was I thinking? If you can't dance, why go to a dance?

I share this to assure the reader that I understand the frustration and embarrassment that can flood one's soul when a fellow believer says, "Can't you just relax and celebrate your Christian-

86

ity? Can't you just turn it all over to God and trust him? Can't you quit worrying and start praising?" While your heart is humming, "Wouldn't It Be Loverly," your brain is singing, "Can't Dance, Don't Ask Me."

One Christian sister put it well. "I wasn't raised with all this happy-clappy, praise-God religion. When we went to church, we heard about how many people were going to hell and how we better watch out or we might end up among them. It's not that I don't want to celebrate my faith; fact is, I just don't think I can."

She is not alone. Christian communities throughout the centuries have found themselves mired in restrictive legalistic approaches to following Jesus that leave little room for celebration. Ascetics in the third century stuffed themselves into hollowed-out tree trunks in attempts to take all the pleasure of sensory input out of life. Puritans in early America thought laughter to be the "sound of the devil's work" and seriousness the true mark of the faithful.

All the while, the heathen orgiests and "party animals" certainly proved that where there was celebration there must be sin. "If it feels good, avoid it!" became the motto of the sensibly, religiously miserable.

What then are we to do with "Rejoice in the Lord . . . always"? Breaking the barriers that keep us from dancing with God in celebration of life is not for the fainthearted. Criticism and pressure will soon come to bear from without and within. When our hearts aren't warning us that our faith is just too much fun, our Christian friends will be. And the danger of losing our focus and allowing freedom in Christ to become a license for licentiousness is a constant concern. But if you'll brave those dangers, there are cures for the maladies that keep us from dancing with the King.

The five diseases of the spirit we'll address in this section are, I believe, the most common; so don't be shocked if you find that you are afflicted with more than one. Most of us will suffer from each one of them at some point in our lives. The good news is that the Great Physician is able to cure them all. The prescriptions are simple and the medicine is easily accessible. But before you go in to see the doctor, know this: You must want to get well. That stipulation is the core of our first celebration-stopper—*Bethesda Blight.*

✦ Bethesda Blight

Now there is in Jerusalem near the Sheep Gate a pool, which in Aramaic is called Bethesda and which is surrounded by five covered colonnades. Here a great number of disabled people used to lie—the blind, the lame, the paralyzed. One who was there had been an invalid for thirty-eight years. (John 5:2–5)

Can you picture this gathering place of the sickly? Day after day folks with every conceivable ailment crawled or limped to this corner of Jerusalem hoping for a miracle. They must have been drawn to the site by local legends—amazing claims that when the angels came and *"stirred"* the water, this otherwise calm pool became a magic Jacuzzi filled with healing powers for whoever jumped in first.

We don't know how many were gathered at the water's edge the day Jesus dropped by, but we do know what they were doing—they were waiting. Without a printed schedule for angelic water stirrings, all they could do was wait . . . and talk. I bet I know what that talk was about.

"Mornin' Ezra, how's your back?"

"Worse than ever. I could barely roll over this morning. And you, Eli?"

"Oy, I wish I could roll over. My legs are like stones—useless!"

"You two should be happy!" another chimes in. "My whole body is stiff as a board. I can't move a muscle!"

"Really? Your mouth doesn't seem to be paralyzed just yet."

I imagine that the moaning and complaining around that pool would make the most pessimistic among us look positively chipper. After months, maybe years, of these daily doses of misery, even the "can-you-top-this" gripe sessions must have lost their luster.

So they lay there, watching the water and waiting.

Into this den of the depressed, comes a true healer. *"When Jesus saw him lying there and learned that he had been in this condition for a long time, he asked him, 'Do you want to get well?'"* (John 5:6).

Did you catch the touch of sarcasm in his question? What could Jesus have been thinking? This poor man had suffered with an inability to move for nearly four decades. No one would actually choose to stay sick, would they? No one would pass up a chance for a full and exuberant lifestyle on purpose!

Or would they?

This paralyzed beggar was struggling with more than just an inability to walk. The best proof of that comes from his own words. The greatest healer of all time asks him if he wants to be well, and what does he say? He makes excuses: *"'Sir,' the invalid replied, 'I have no one to help me into the pool when the water is stirred. While I am trying to get in, someone else goes down ahead of me'"* (John 5:7).

Now is it just me, or did this guy miss the point? All he had to say was, "Sure, I want to be healed! In fact, right now would be great!"

> ◆
>
> More than just his legs had become paralyzed. He had lost the expectation of a different life.
>
> ◆

But it seems that more than just his legs had become paralyzed. He had lost the expectation of a different life. This was his lot, and he had accepted it. Coming to the pool and watching for the angels' presence was just a way to pass a Sabbath. And Jesus sees it. His question underlines the man's need: He had to start by truly seeking something more—not just talking or griping, but really seeking.

When this kind of paralysis of expectations occurs in the spiritual realm, it's even more pathetic. The soul sicknesses that keep us from joyfully celebrating our salvation in Christ can become comfortable excuses. Whether it is sin, doubt, or fear that holds us back from opening our hearts fully to God's grace and joy, the excuses all start sounding alike. The words may vary, but the tune's the same:

"It's just not my nature."

"I'm just not made that way."

"I've always been like this."

"It doesn't feel comfortable."

"I wasn't raised like that."

If this sounds familiar, you may have just discovered your first dance-inhibiting disease. But like our paralyzed friend by the pool, Jesus is never far away from those looking for his help to change.

✦ Balms for the Blighted Soul

The Bethesda Blight isn't conquered with a lecture on dancing or a seminar on rejoicing. Its pain is best relieved with some deep-heating rubs that will warm your insides and rekindle your hope for more passionate faith. In particular, I recommend three specific biblical ointments that can limber up your spirit for the high-stepping celebration to which God invites you. Start with a handful of each, and rub them in thoroughly.

The Salve of a Sublime Vision

Like the paralytic at the Bethesda pool, we, too, may be unable to envision the possibilities. How can we hope for a richer, fuller walk with Christ if we have no concept of what to hope for? In order to experience a more joyous, celebrative life in the Lord, you must first see it with the eyes of your heart. Like the pole vaulter who can envision himself sailing over a bar set at world record heights or the runner who imagines breaking the tape at the head of the pack, getting and believing a vision of what you desire in your spiritual life impassions and empowers your quest.

Some have called this "seeing the reaching" and others simply "clarifying your target." The language you use matters little; but the clarity of your vision matters greatly. Can you see yourself worshiping God with a passion equal to that felt at the most joyous event in your life? Can you imagine spending time in such fervent prayer that the Lord's presence with you was almost tangible?

Visions have been used by God throughout history to raise the expectations and deepen the faith of his people. But turning a vision into reality is no easy task. Years of lackluster worship and monotonous praise can take the edge of expectancy off of our faith. Seeking something more in our spiritual walk can even feel blasphemous, as though God might be offended that we would want a deeper, more moving faith experience. Yet the Bible itself encourages us to think big, for we have a God who thinks bigger than we ever could: *"Now to him who is able to do immeasurably more than all we ask or imagine, according to his power that is at work within us, to him be glory in the church and in Christ Jesus throughout all generations, for ever and ever! Amen"* (Ephesians 3:20–21).

✦

> But turning a vision into reality is no easy task. Years of lackluster worship and monotonous praise can take the edge of expectancy off of our faith.

✦

Go ahead, raise the expectation level in your heart. Imagine a passionate relationship with God that moves you to tears as well as laughter. Envision a deeper faith that wipes away the paralysis of doubt and enables more powerful witnessing and more courageous service than you've ever known. See the believer you want to be.

But don't stop there. Try a bit of this next ointment on those aching muscles.

The Ointment of an Optimistic Faith

"God can."

If I could have two words printed on the back of my eyelids that I might see them every time I blink, it would be those: "God can." Satan's lies from the dawn of mankind have all been derivatives of denying that truth. He knows that doubt is the soft spot in our faith:

"God won't punish you."

"God can't help you."

"God won't find out."

"God just doesn't do that anymore."

Whether slithering around Eden or barging into the courts of heaven to challenge Job's commitment, the devil's only hope of victory is to convince man of these falsehoods. And I'll be the first to admit, he can be awfully effective at times. I've heard that little voice inside my own head, even as I'm praying and asking God for healing or some other blessing: "You know he's not gonna do it. Go ahead and make yourself feel good by praying . . . but you know it ain't gonna happen. Not in this life, Pal."

Even with a graphic vision of what life could be firmly planted in my heart, I'm still paralyzed and powerless if I don't believe that God can and will do it. Remember, it is his power, not mine, that will set me dancing. Faith in his ability and willingness to act on my behalf is what separates those fearfully hugging the wall from those striding onto the floor, trusting the Lord to provide the music and the movement. Again the apostle Paul's pen gives us the confidence we seek: *"I can do everything through him who gives me strength"* (Philippians 4:13).

Paul's faith is not in his own ability, but in the power and willingness of God. Whatever you may be told, know this: *God can.* He can give you more joy. He can set you free from guilt and fear. He can melt your inhibitions and set your feet to tapping. He *can*, so rub that in deep!

The final prescription may be the most potent: apply liberal doses of the balm of boldness!

The Balm of Boldness

The signature moment in the musical adaptation of Charles Dickens' *Oliver Twist* involves a boy and a bowl. Oliver is living in an orphanage run by stingy and cruel overseers who dole out nothing but meager portions of gruel at every meal. All the hungry orphans eat their mush in silence—all except Oliver. He finishes his bowlful and then dares to walk up to the headmaster and utter two words: "More, please?" Those in charge are so shocked at his insolence that Oliver is beaten and ejected from the orphanage posthaste while they sing, "Who would dare to ask for *more?*"

♦

Equating boldness with sinfulness is not unique to nineteenth-century English orphanages. Many Christians buy into the philosophy that timidity and holiness go hand in hand. They think that the quiet believer who dutifully goes through his days, never daring to ask for anything more in his relationship with God, is somehow ennobled through his contentment. "Isn't it brash to ask God for more?" some ask. "Shouldn't we be content with the life we've been given?"

Boldness born of self-confidence or selfish desire can indeed lead to sin. The bragging conceit of the egotistical Christian who thinks that the spiritual universe revolves around his needs and wants is clearly not pleasing to God. But boldness rooted in a desire to be all that God calls us to be and experience all he offers cannot be despised.

> Many Christians think that the quiet believer who never dares to ask for anything more is somehow ennobled through his contentment.

The early Christians actually prayed and asked God for more boldness so that they might face the threats of the enemy with confidence (Acts 4:29). And the apostle Paul cautions his young son in the faith about swallowing the kind of logic that equates timidity with spirituality: *"For God did not give us a spirit of timidity, but a spirit of power, of love and of self-discipline"* (2 Timothy 1:7). Moreover, boldness is required not only to experience deeper intimacy and greater celebration with God, but also to share that newfound thrill with others. If we hide behind the timid excuse, "I can't!" we will never know the joy he offers, and we will never be the witness the world needs.

♦

If given the choice, they'd take a safe walk with Christ over a surprising dance with him, any day.

♦

But boldness does not come without risk. As the famous captain of the starship Enterprise knew, "boldly going where no man has gone before" means facing some weird creatures in bizarre circumstances. The comfort of the familiar is replaced with the challenge of the new and different. Old answers to tough questions are less satisfying, and new experiences bring their own puzzles.

At its root, the problem for many is the fear of the unknown. When some say, "I can't dance," they are really saying, "I'm afraid of what will happen if I do." They stand frozen, unprepared to turn loose and let God be God. Don't expect them to put it in those terms; but if given the choice, they'd take a safe walk with Christ over a surprising dance with him, any day. But miracles and life without limits are only available in the realm of the unexpected, the jubilant, the outrageous. As in music, the ad-lib sections are always the most exciting . . . if you're ready for them.

My long-time friend, Rick, shares a story about his experience one summer with a junior high jazz band that explains it better than I could:

> Being chosen to play third trumpet in the Bakersfield All City Jazz Orchestra was an honor. Most of the other kids were older and had been playing jazz for quite a while. I felt so cool that first day as I found my chair. I sat

94

down and began warming up my mouthpiece and thinking about the summer ahead. The music we were to play was all jazz—no classics allowed. We were even scheduled to do a full-blown, big-band concert in a city auditorium in August. This was gonna be the best summer of my life! Just then, Jack Miner walked to the band leader's stand. He was the new jazz band teacher from the high school. He was sharp, he was young, he was single, and he was the very definition of "hip." He stepped to the podium and got right to it.

"I know you're all here to play jazz, so I won't waste your time by talking. Let's start with chart number six. Trumpets will take the ad-lib solos. About this fast: one, two, a-one two three four." And we were off. He was snapping his fingers in rhythm with one hand and punching the air with his other on the off beats. He looked like something straight out of the big-band era. And the band sounded great! My third trumpet part was fairly easy— just straight eighth notes—so I played it with gusto. This was the life. I imagined that Mr. Miner was Doc Severinsen and that I was the star trumpeter. I just knew I looked cool, swinging my horn as I hit those off-beat eighth notes. Then, half-way through the second page, Mr. Miner pointed at the first-chair trumpet, and the whole band quit playing while he stood and began a solo. I listened enraptured to the wild music he was making, but when I looked for it on the page, all I found were two Latin words—*"Ad Lib."* Mr. Miner was grinning and saying, "Yeah, man, go!" and bouncing along with the beat.

"Where'd he get the music?" I asked the second-chair trumpet as the first trumpet finished his solo and Mr. Miner swung the band right back into the refrain we had been playing.

"He made it up. That's ad-libbing."

Wow. Ad-libbing. What a cool thing. I was wondering how long it had taken him to learn to do that, but before I could ask any more questions, another section of the tune was finished and Mr. Miner was pointing to the second-chair trumpeter. He stood and began to wail his own solo. I'm sure his ad-libbing was just as hot as the first chair's had been, but I confess, I wasn't able to enjoy it.

Sweat had begun cascading off my brow. My palms were soaked, and my lips had gone numb. Every time Mr. Miner said "Go, man, go," my heart skipped three beats. I may have been naive and even unprepared, but I could count, for goodness sake!!! Third chair would be next. I couldn't do that! Not here, not in front of all these people. But the band just kept playing, and I had nowhere to run.

Four measures, and my life was going to be over. Three. Two. One. And then Mr. Miner pointed at me.

My legs froze. I couldn't stand. My teeth were locked behind my mouthpiece. It was all I could do to stay conscious. Every eye turned toward me, and then, somehow, I stood and played.

Well, actually, I tried to play.

◆

My legs froze. My teeth were locked behind my mouthpiece. It was all I could do to stay conscious.

◆

What came out were three short blurps and one high bleeeeep. The last note sounded like a cross between a bad kazoo and a sick llama. Needless to say, I didn't get so much as a "Yeah, man," from Mr. Miner. He just shook his head and counted the band back into the last refrain of the tune.

I sat down, took the mouthpiece from my trumpet, and packed them both back in the case. Then as the band finished the song, I quietly slipped out of the only rehearsal I would ever attend for the Bakersfield All City Jazz Orchestra.

I can't read that story without hurting for my friend. No one had told him what would be expected. No one had warned him that a moment would come when he would be in the spotlight, when he'd have a shot at doing his own thing. And though he managed to make it through that emotional trauma, he missed the chance to play his big solo.

But don't ever say nobody warned *you:* Life is not a series of straight eighth notes. God gives each of us moments to take the stage and boldly play our song. Whether in exultant praise or solemn testimony, the Christian must be ready for the unexpected chance to dance with the King. And he must step out with boldness to do it!

Well, there they are: three tonics good for what ails you. I advise you to take these medicinal rubs, and not be skimpy with them. With a sublime vision in your mind, an optimistic faith in your soul, and boldness in your heart, you can get past the paralyzing *can't*s of life and onto the dance floor of the Divine.

When you do, your final results can be as blessed as the paralyzed man by the pool. *"Then Jesus said to him, 'Get up! Pick up your mat and walk.' At once the man was cured; he picked up his mat and walked"* . . . and soon, no doubt, he danced for joy! Doesn't that sound like a new experience worth having?

Or in the words of Jesus, *"Do you want to get well?"*

*A*S Jesus and his disciples were on their way, he came to a village where a woman named Martha opened her home to him. She had a sister called Mary, who sat at the Lord's feet listening to what he said. But Martha was distracted by all the preparations that had to be made. She came to him and asked, "Lord, don't you care that my sister has left me to do the work by myself? Tell her to help me!"

"Martha, Martha," the Lord answered, "you are worried and upset about many things, but only one thing is needed. Mary has chosen what is better and it will not be taken away from her."

✦ Luke 10:38–42

7

Marthaplexy –
The Workaholic's Twitch

"Can't Dance with
My Apron On"

Well I'm tired and so weary, but I must move along
Till the Lord comes to call me away.

from the song, "Peace in the Valley"

Been there recently? You know the spot. It's somewhere between exhausted and burnt-out. The place where you go when all you want to do is lie down and quit. If that appeals to you, maybe it's time you learned to take your apron off and dance.

I must begin by confessing that I know the spot mentioned above rather well. Put it this way: I can get around without a map. I could show you Griper's Corner, a nice shady place to sit and complain about how hard you are working and how little everyone else is, or Doubters Drive, a crooked little street that's perfect for strolling along while you wonder if anything you do really matters. Then there's the Pity Pool, deep and black, a great spot at which to shed tears over lack of appreciation and recognition. Oh yes, I'm a regular . . . or at least, I used to be.

And the place was always crowded.

Just cruise past the personal devotional shelf in your local Christian bookstore and count the titles mentioning stress, guilt, or burnout. You better take a calculator. For many, the exuberance and delight with which they first greeted Christ quickly fizzles. Life in Christ becomes a holy rut, a righteous routine. It's almost as if they have gone spiritually numb. All that remains of the initial thrill is a constant drive to be better and do more. I cannot count the number of Christian friends and acquaintances who have reported experiencing this same malady. I call it *Marthaplexy*, named after its most famous victim.

✦ A Tale of Two Sisters

Consider the plight of Ms. M.—the hard-working, ultimately dedicated follower of Christ. When the church doors were open, she was there. And you wouldn't find her sitting around chatting. No, more likely you'd catch fleeting glimpses of her in the kitchen getting things ready for the afternoon potluck. She was a tireless dynamo. Director of VBS, overseer of the nursery ministry, and leader of the Ladies Service League . . . until the day it all caught up with her. One minute she was lovingly serving the Lord and the next she was tattling on her sister and ordering Jesus to give her a spanking!

"Lord, don't you care that my sister has left me to do the work by myself? Tell her to help me!" (Luke 10:40). There are few things as annoying as having to work while others play. My little brother used to take special delight in sitting on the porch and criticizing

while I mowed the lawn. He could always get my goat with comments like, "You missed a spot over by the tree. Better go over that again!" It wasn't just that he pointed out my mistakes that bothered me so, it was that he wouldn't lift a finger to help! But in Martha's case, her irritation may have been less with Mary than with Jesus. "Why didn't he tell Mary to get with it?" Martha must have wondered. But did you notice his response to Martha? " 'Martha, Martha,' the Lord answered, 'you are worried and upset about many things, but only one thing is needed.' "

He gives her the correction she was lining up for Mary. I imagine she didn't even see it coming. I mean, what could Jesus possibly want to correct her for? She was the busy, productive organized member of this little household. I guess she hadn't spotted the symptoms of the savage sickness she carried. The description contained in *Henry's Handy Handbook of Spiritual Diseases* is pretty concise:

Marthaplexy

A nervous disorder of the spirit, causing almost constant fits of religious activity leading to intense fatigue and total loss of joy. (Sometimes referred to as *Elijah Complex.*)

Symptoms

• *Chronic fatigue*

Periods of intense activity followed by extreme tiredness and excessive guilt. Watch for phrases like, "I just don't have time to get it all done!" and "I'm the only one who can do it." Vacations and time off are often postponed or curtailed. Sleep habits may be disrupted, and long periods of activity will be followed with a "crash-and-burn" syndrome.

• *Heightened critical tendencies*

Marked increase in criticism of others, especially those who appear truly joyful. Critical comments are often leveled at those closest. Family members should watch for sneers and smirks when discussing spiritual needs. Also be alert to an interest and increase in repeating bad news. It may appear at times that the subject actually enjoys hearing of problems in the lives of others.

• *Loss of interest in praise*
Dramatic decrease in praise language. Subject may actually take offense at others praising God for good things. Prayers will virtually exclude giving thanks, except for mentions of rest in heaven. (See following symptom.)

• *Increased focus on rewards in heaven*
Watch for repeated singing or humming of "Swing Low, Sweet Chariot" or "We'll Work Till Jesus Comes." Discussions will often rise over what heaven will be like, with an emphasis on rest. Oddly, though, these discussions will often be followed with statements that question the subject's fitness for eternity, i.e., "I just pray that I've done enough."

Comments
In the early stages, the disease can seem quite helpful. The subject will be most likely to volunteer for any religious or pious work and will head charity committees and serve on coordinating boards. Subject will outserve those not afflicted and appear to enjoy doing so, but as the disease progresses, bitteress, resentment, and short-temperedness often set in. If not treated at this stage, complete dissatisfaction with other Christians can lead to disassociation from the local church and possible total loss of faith. (*Warning:* Constant association with an infected person can lead to intense irritation and possible infection.)

Sounds like our friend, Martha, all right, and like a lot of other Christian folk who have missed the invitation to dance with God because they are so busy getting ready to entertain him. Like Martha, they may have confused the preparation with the party, for they swallow two infectious lies that keep folks like her off the divine dance floor.

Lie #1: Working Is More Important Than Dancing

Who could argue with that? Certainly not our modern-day Marthas. They know that God has gifted them and called them to serve. They've heard enough sermons on the parable of the talents to insure that they will never be caught burying one. They may die early, as religious stress is particularly hard on the heart, but they won't pass up an opportunity to do good. It just wouldn't be right.

This kind of spiritual workaholism is kept alive by the constant calls for greater discipleship issued from all corners of American Christiandom. Admittedly, believers in the United States may have a tendency toward spiritual laziness due, in part, to our prosperity. We fear no government authorities when we assemble, and since our Christian faith appears to cost so little, we often value it similarly. But our temporal blessings don't mean that we are condemned to earning our salvation by the sweat we no longer expend in the cotton fields. Celebrating and enjoying the gift of grace is an important "task," to use language most familiar to workaholics.

God made this truth plain to Israel from the beginning. When he revealed through Moses the story of creation in Genesis, what did he place at the finale of his great work? A day off. And not because he needed it. God modeled for man the importance of a day to rest, to relax, and to dance! His later written ordinances made the purpose crystal clear.

> *Observe the Sabbath, because it is holy to you. Anyone who desecrates it must be put to death; whoever does any work on that day must be cut off from his people. For six days work is to be done, but the seventh day is a Sabbath of rest, holy to the Lord. Whoever does any work on the Sabbath day must be put to death. The Israelites are to observe the Sabbath, celebrating it for the generations to come as a lasting covenant.* (Exodus 31:14–16)

103

The Sabbath was serious business. Violating it brought the same punishment as adultery or murder. It was to be celebrated by Israel because God decreed that a day of rest and rejuvenation was holy to the Lord. And God didn't stop with just a weekly observance. He decreed that there would be regular Sabbath times of celebration and festivity throughout the year. Feasts and festivals were scheduled into Israel's calendar right along with planting and harvest. Whether they liked it or not, Israel was to take time from work to dance with God several times a year. Why?

First, God knew we needed it. Without these forced breaks from daily work, man's greed would drive him to work without ceasing. Slaves would know no respite, and soon, work would be king. The health ramifications of overwork are all around us, but the spiritual results are less evident. When time is not taken to relax and dance the dance of stillness with God, the moral fortress of the heart grows weak. Work takes on the aura of holiness, and we come to believe that our work is essential to the future of the universe, that the world won't spin another centimeter if we aren't out there doing our bit. Ultimately, our fantasy is that God *needs* our work. If we don't do it, who will?

Second, an emphasis on relaxation and rest helps us guard against spiritual egotism. Without pauses for rejuvenation and reflection on God, our own labors become the center of our faith. Thinking like that delights Satan, for it elevates the position of man. We become little princes, ruling our religious kingdoms and determining our futures by the sweat of our brows. And if we can handle our futures, we can set our own laws, morals, and codes of honor. We'll decide how success is judged and what part ethics play, if any. If the ends are profit and growth, especially in the religious realm, then any means will be considered holy. Only the demand of God that we lay down our Daytimers and just celebrate his goodness can cut through that kind of fraudulent reasoning.

Lie #2: Working Makes You Holy; Dancing Just Makes You Feel Good

This second lie may come closest to the reason behind Martha's outburst. Maybe it was the smile on Mary's face that finally caused her to snap, for Mary was surely smiling as she sat at the feet of the Lord; and Martha surely wasn't. When you fall prey to the "work makes you righteous" mind-set, anyone who seems genuinely happy is a real irritant. *"How dare they sit there and grin; that just proves they don't know what's going on around here."* Martha, like many, may have come to accept her own miserableness as just the way it's supposed to be. I can describe it best by sharing an experience from my first ski trip.

Though I'd never been skiing, I had listened to my college friends gush with enthusiasm about the sport for years. They showed me alluring photos from ski magazines that made the whole thing look exciting and glamorous. But I was thoroughly unimpressed. The thought of paying good money to be out in the freezing cold with a strong chance of fracturing a limb wasn't my idea of a nice Easter *break*. But soon, I found myself wondering what it would be like to fly down a snow-clad mountainside . . . with a trail of thirty ski bunnies behind me. So one April I gave in. Fortunately, there were a few other novices on the trip, including my close friend, Rick. He and I decided to spend the first day in ski lessons so we wouldn't stand out, or rather *fall* out, in front of the more advanced members of our group.

♦

When you fall prey to the "work makes you righteous" mind-set, anyone who seems genuinely happy is a real irritant.

♦

Skiing is 90 percent equipment. You get the right boots and skis and you're in for a real treat. So we took our time getting fitted.

"Are they good and tight?" the girl at the rental shop asked us as she locked me into some flaming red ski boots.

"Oh yeah, they're plenty snug," I replied, already feeling an adrenaline rush at just seeing my feet in those high-tech rockets. Rick agreed that his were tight too. All suited up, we headed off to ski lessons. Mercifully, the sun was out and the weather was gorgeous, because our skiing was hideous. I never imagined that simply remaining upright could be such a difficult task. As I fell for the fifty-first time, I told myself, "This is the price you pay to end up with the ski bunnies." And sure enough, before the day was over, we were both getting down the slopes, more or less in one piece. The last run was a classic. The snow was great, the wind was whipping by, and I made it all the way down without falling. I was hooked.

After skiing, we returned to the "chalet" our group had rented. (It looked like a cabin to me, but my skiing friends quickly set me straight.) We changed into comfy clothes and started swapping stories of the day's great runs. It was then that Rick came downstairs. He had taken a longer shower than the rest of us, so we were all there to witness his amazing decent. He'd taken off both his shoes and was gripping the stair rails for all he was worth. He seemed to be trying his best not to touch the stairs with his feet as he came down. The end effect was that he looked like an old man walking on hot coals . . . with a bad case of arthritis. When he finally managed to settle into a chair, he announced that he was never going skiing again. When asked why, he just pulled off his socks and pointed to his toes. Both big toes were black, and it looked as though he would surely lose the nails. "Rick! What happened to your feet!" I asked.

"What do you mean, 'What happened?' The *boots* happened. Didn't your feet hurt?" he responded with a frown.

"Of course not. Your boots must have been way too small. Why didn't you say something?"

I'll never forget his sheepish response. "I thought your feet were supposed to hurt."

I'm convinced that many of us become just like that—silent, miserable Christians who've accepted the lie that Christianity is supposed to hurt. If it feels good, it can't be right. We assume it is the will of the Father that our faith feel as cramped and uncomfortable as a pair of bad boots. We leave the happiness to the heathens while we bravely march on. No time for dancing here. Let's have stiff upper lips and another chorus of "Farther along we'll know all about it." It's amazing how heaven takes on such meaning when your Christian life feels like hell.

So what's a Martha to do? In that question lies part of the remedy: doing isn't the answer.

✦ The Dance of Stillness

The dance to which God invites the Martha in all of us is a quiet one. It is the restful, easy tempo found in silence, the gentle rhythm of peace. The psalmist danced to it often, for he knew God was there.

> *Be still before the Lord and wait patiently for him;*
>   *do not fret when men succeed in their ways,*
>   *when they carry out their wicked schemes.*
> (Psalm 37:7)

And again,

> *Be still, and know that I am God;*
>   *I will be exalted among the nations,*
>   *I will be exalted in the earth.*
> (Psalm 46:10)

Stillness of soul and body is hard to come by for those of us given to chronic busyness. Its value is hidden by our productivity-tinted glasses. "Sabbath" can sound so outdated and "meditation" too Eastern. Yet God patiently invites us again and again with that still, small voice to a place where, like Elijah, we will come to our senses in a moment of clarifying stillness. In that stillness, we can once again see the glory of God and bask in his power. We can be caught up in the blessed reality of his sovereignty and our servitude.

But that place is not found without discipline. The same dogged determination that we apply to our religious work must be turned toward seeking frequent times of rest and quiet. Space must be carved out of an already crowded schedule for waiting upon the Lord. Vacations and mini-get-aways must become regular events.

And even these must be monitored to make sure that real Sabbath is occurring. I only realized how out of control my own Marthaplexy had become when my wife described my vacation style as "You hurry up and go, so you can hurry up and get back." Even trips to Disneyland were marked by constant rushing to the tune of, "We've got thirty minutes to get in three more rides!" I'm convinced we behave like this because most of us overwait for times of respite, and then we try to cram a month's peace into two weeks of hectic vacationing. Peace must be found in little pieces—a quiet walk after dinner or an early morning time of reading and meditating—which introduces another key ingredient: prayer.

✦

Rather than bombarding God with our list of needs and wants, we must allow prayer to define our position of surrender.

✦

Prayer time must move from the "When Available" column to the "Must Do Today" list. And the very nature of that prayer must change. Rather than bombarding God with our list of needs and wants, we must allow prayer to redefine our position of surrender and affirm the Father's control. In one of the longest recorded prayers in the Old Testament, the prophet Daniel repeatedly affirmed God's paramount position: *"I prayed to the Lord my God and confessed: 'O Lord, the great and awesome God, who keeps his covenant of love with all who love him and obey his commands, we have sinned and done wrong'"* (Daniel 9:4–5).

Through his prayer, Daniel reminded himself of the power and might of the Lord. In doing so, he declared not only God's supremacy but his own dependence. Even Jesus, in his darkest hour when so much depended on his choices, prayed his own confirmation of the Father's sovereignty: *"Not my will, but yours be done."* The Scriptures are full of metaphors that can aid us in our prayer process: He is the shepherd; we are the sheep. He is the vine; we are the branches. He is the potter; we are the clay. Permeating our prayers with these visual images can make communing with God a release for the pent-up stress and guilt that can steal our desire to dance.

So instead of throwing another stone into the Pity Pool, why not visit the quiet place where God waits to dance the dance of stillness with us? Once you've relearned those steps, you'll be ready for the more joyous dances of celebration and praise!

NOW one of the Pharisees invited Jesus to have dinner with him, so he went to the Pharisee's house and reclined at the table. When a woman who had lived a sinful life in that town learned that Jesus was eating at the Pharisee's house, she brought an alabaster jar of perfume, and as she stood behind him at his feet weeping, she began to wet his feet with her tears. Then she wiped them with her hair, kissed them and poured perfume on them. . . .

When the Pharisee who had invited him saw this, he said to himself, "If this man were a prophet, he would know who is touching him and what kind of woman she is—that she is a sinner."

Then he turned toward the woman and said to Simon, "Do you see this woman? I came into your house. You did not give me any water for my feet, but she wet my feet with her tears and wiped them with her hair. You did not give me a kiss, but this woman, from the time I entered, has not stopped kissing my feet. You did not put oil on my head, but she has poured perfume on my feet. Therefore, I tell you, her many sins have been forgiven—for she loved much. But he who has been forgiven little loves little."

✦ Luke 7:36–39, 44–47

Simonosis — Rigor Mortis of the Spirit

"My Shoes Are Too Tight"

We got a new "amen-er" at the church where I serve. It had been a while since we'd had one, so it caught everyone a bit off guard on that first Sunday. I was just getting into my sermon when I mentioned in passing that salvation was a marvelous gift. *"Amen! That's true!"* boomed from the back of the auditorium. Heads snapped. Hymnbooks fell. I tried not to let it throw me off. "Yet there are many," I continued, "who take this marvelous gift for granted." *"Oh me, that's right!"* responded the voice from the back. At that point I knew I was in for an exciting Sunday. His spontaneous contributions to the sermon continued, and by the time the morning was over, everyone was all abuzz.

111

"Who is that guy?" Well, we found out when he and his whole family placed membership. Over the next few weeks, I learned to anticipate the "Oh me's" and the "Yeah, that's rights." I even tried to leave him room to squeeze them in after points I thought he'd especially appreciate. "I hope you don't mind my 'Amens,'" he said one Sunday after a particularly stirring lesson. "I just can't sit there and say nothing when the truth is so good. I just have to express it!"

His words rang in my ears and reminded me of Paul's admonition to the Galatian Christians. It seems they were getting conflicting reports about the basis for their salvation. Some Jewish Christian leaders were suggesting that only through strict obedience to the Old Testament law, as well as following Jesus Christ, could one be saved. Anyone who had not been circumcised and was not keeping all the Hebrew ordinances and rituals was displeasing to God. The apostle's response left no doubt about his position in the debate . . . nor about God's.

> It is for freedom that Christ has set us free. Stand firm, then, and do not let yourselves be burdened again by a yoke of slavery. Mark my words! I, Paul, tell you that if you let yourselves be circumcised, Christ will be of no value to you at all. . . . For in Christ Jesus neither circumcision nor uncircumcision has any value. The only thing that counts is faith expressing itself through love. (Galatians 5:1–2, 6)

Did you catch that last phrase? "Faith expressing itself through love." There is something fundamentally wrong with a faith that isn't ever expressed. The meaning of the word connotes letting something out that is inside, as in "expressing your feelings." Though the style may vary, expressions of faith and joy in Christ have long been part of the fabric of Christian worship. I remember growing up in a church where hardly a Sunday would pass without someone saying "Amen." But in some religious circles, these spontaneous expressions of faith have become so metered and subdued that they are almost nonexistent.

Think about it: When was the last time you *hallelujah*ed any-thing—a sermon, a song, a sunrise? Don't limit your thinking only to the worship assembly. Whether it was riding in the car or sitting in a small group, when last did you let your inner faith in God's goodness bubble out in an expression that could be seen and heard by others?

If that question threatens or disturbs you, it may be that your shoes are just a bit too tight for you to enjoy dancing with the King. Simon's certainly were. His uptight and critical attitudes prompted me to dub the disease he struggled with *Simonosis*. His story is worth our time.

We meet Simon in the seventh chapter of Luke's gospel: *"Now one of the Pharisees invited Jesus to have dinner with him, so he went to the Pharisee's house and reclined at the table."*

Who was this fellow, Simon? The text tells us little about him, except that he was a Pharisee. That clues us in to his place in soci-ety and his feelings about the law. But what might his next-door neighbor say? "This guy is one serious religious type! I mean, you ain't going to catch him messing around outside after the sun goes down on Friday. When the Sabbath hits, he's where he should be, doing what he ought to be doing. And don't offer him a bacon, let-tuce, and tomato sandwich, either—he's Kosher through and through! The man is kosher through and through. Why, I don't think he'd take a shower without his prayer shawl on, he's just that kind of guy!"

Sounds impressive. A dedicated and scrupulously proper Hebrew. What's more, in wanting to keep abreast of the latest trends on the radical fringes of his faith, he invites the young upstart new rabbi, Jesus, over for dinner. Now this must have posed some challenges that had to be handled delicately. He was going to have this Jesus sitting at the same table with all his Phar-isee buddies. Everything would have to be perfect. The food must be twice blessed, the house spotless, and the table settings just right. It would be a black-tie-and-toga affair. You know the feeling, like the last time you had your in-laws over, the ones who come equipped with a white glove and magnifying glass. As a minister, I finally quit calling ahead when I went to visit people. I found out that in some homes the prior notice was causing a huge commotion. Mom would race around picking up the house, while Dad hunted for the family Bible to lay on the coffee table.

But Simon would have had everything in its place. He had probably even mapped out the conversation in his mind: "We'll chat a little about Isaiah, maybe some Haggai. I'll get his opinion on the new Roman prelate, and then we'll get to the root of these miracle rumors that are flying around about him." Even though Simon may have covered every base in his preparations, nothing could have readied him for what would happen soon after the meal began. *"When a woman who had lived a sinful life in that town learned that Jesus was eating at the Pharisee's house, she brought an alabaster jar of perfume, and as she stood behind him at his feet weeping . . . "* (Luke 7:37–38).

It's definitely Pepto-Bismol time at Simon's house. Into the middle of his carefully orchestrated dinner party comes . . . a hussy. A woman, the Scripture says, *"who had lived a sinful life."* She had to be the very last person Simon wanted showing up at his little soirée. You've got to believe the poor guy is in agony. How had she even gotten wind that Jesus was there? I guarantee you, she did not get an invitation in the mail with a map enclosed! But there she stood, nonetheless. Take a good look at her—she's weeping, emotionally out of control. She clearly doesn't belong here, and she's gushing her feelings all over the floor. This lady was outlandish! She was eccentric! She was unconventional! She was excessive!

And she was everything Simon wasn't.

How would he react? Something tells me his first instinct would be: "If I just ignore her, she'll go away. I'll bring out some more dip, have another glass of wine, and when I turn around, she'll be gone. We'll move on to dessert, and it will be over. After all, it can't get any worse, can it?"

But of course, it could, and it did. *"She began to wet his feet with her tears. Then she wiped them with her hair, kissed them and poured perfume on them."*

Okay. We've gone way over the edge now! Being seen in the same room with a woman like her was social suicide. But to have her massaging your guest's feet? Wetting them with her tears? Drying them with her hair? Simon was feeling sick, "Somebody call an ambulance; I think I feel a coronary coming on!" But just before the room began to spin, it dawned on him: "Wait. This is perfect! How could I have missed it?" Simon suddenly began to see this woman not as an irksome intruder but as a beautiful trap. The Scriptures reveal his thoughts: *"When the Pharisee who had invited him saw this, he said to himself, 'If this man were a prophet, he would know who is touching him and what kind of woman she is—that she is a sinner.'"*

Here was the proof Simon needed to dismiss this Messiah wanna-be once and for all. No prophet worth his salt would let a woman touch him in public, much less one with a questionable background. If he had only been able to keep those thoughts to himself, the story might have ended right there. But ironically, while Simon was smugly thinking that Jesus could not read this woman's heart, Jesus was busy reading Simon's. As the text points out, the Lord responded to the question Simon didn't verbalize: *"Jesus answered him, 'Simon, I have something to tell you.'"*

And with that, Jesus told Simon a simple story—a parable, actually, about two debtors. One owed a great deal, another only a small amount. Neither of them had the money to repay their debts, so their creditor graciously canceled them. *"Now which of them,"* Jesus asks Simon, *"will love him more?"* Simon must have thought

◆

While Simon was smugly thinking that Jesus could not read this woman's heart, Jesus was busy reading Simon's.

◆

115

only a moment before he answered, "The one who had the greater debt forgiven."

Now, I would like to give Simon enough credit to think that at this point, he saw where Jesus was heading. I would like to say that the metaphor sunk in. I would like to say that Simon immediately understood the principle Jesus was illustrating. I would like to say that . . . but I can't. Like most of us, Simon was too busy trying to make sure he was getting all his religious i's dotted and his t's crossed to see the truth. So Christ made sure he saw it.

"Simon, do you see this woman?" Jesus asked him.

Now that was a silly question. What do you think he had been staring at for the last ten minutes? Of course he saw her. Or did he? Jesus wanted Simon to get a good, long look. He wanted him to stare into the face of someone who was unafraid to boldly express her faith in love. If we freeze the picture right here, we may have the best comparison and contrast example you could ask for.

On the one hand, we have Simon—buttoned-down and proper, careful and conservative, sanctified and subdued.

On the other hand, we have the woman—outlandish and loud, showy and demonstrative, emotional and expressive.

And which one did the Lord commend?

✦ Simonosis

Before we tackle the cure for Simon's narrow-minded blindness, let's make sure we understand the disease—for we, too, may be afflicted. The open and demonstrative expression of love that the woman poured out at Jesus' feet came from her heart. But we must be ever wary of thinking that we can read the heart of another believer simply through their outward acts and expressions. Have you ever been to a wedding and heard a bride blubber through her vows? She's barely able to get out the "I, Judy, take thee, Willie . . . " because she's so consumed by her emotions and feelings. By the time she finishes up with "till death do us part," every woman in the church is weeping into a handkerchief and saying, "Isn't this just *beautiful*." Then it's the groom's turn. Without so much as a quiver in his lip, he plows right through the vows with all the emotion of a lump of cottage cheese, "I, Willie, take thee, Judy, to be my wedded wife. . . ." And all those women are thinking, "That big lummox! Doesn't he even care? He doesn't even mean those words! Oh, I'm worried about this marriage."

But they can no more judge poor emotionless Willie's sincerity by his tone of voice than they can judge Judy's devotion by the tears on her cheek. God sees the heart, and he alone is the judge. Just because I shout "Hallelujah!" out loud or say "Amen" every third sentence doesn't guarantee my spiritual authenticity.

Have we all got that?

However . . . if you go through your married life without expressing your love passionately, if you never weep over the joy of loving or laugh out loud at the wonder of life itself, what's holding you back? If you go through the Christian life, never crying about the sacrifice of the Savior and never audibly saying "hallelujah" about the gift of salvation, what keeps you from it?

Could it be that we have trained ourselves to rein in all that feeling? Could it be that we're so concerned and worried about praising God in the right way, at the right time, that we end up not praising him at all? Our phobia about expressing our feelings makes our praise as dry and passionless as a saltine cracker . . . and just about that moving to an observer.

When I listen to Jesus' comments to Simon, his message is clear. "Let me tell you something about people who love me a lot. They're extravagant. They're generous. They pour out whatever they have, and they do it in front of anyone who will watch."

Simply put, Christ calls us to praise him with abandon. Moreover, consider four losses we suffer when we put our passion in a bottle and keep it there.

It Removes Your Joy

It's hard to enjoy the party when you're worrying about whether every glass has a coaster under it or if someone will spill punch on the carpet. Simon-like thinking drives Christians to become little Gospel Gestapos, ever on patrol lest someone do or say something that's not exactly as they think it should be. Driven by a fear of anything that's new and a reverence for everything that's middle-of-the-road, people with this mind-set can't be comfortable turning loose of their inhibitions and singing at the top of their lungs or raising their hands in spontaneous praise. It might get out of hand, you see. Someone might just break open her alabaster jar right here . . . and then what would we have? These folks would have pulled the woman in Luke's account aside and said, "Honey, why don't you just leave that box here for Jesus with a little note that says, 'This is for you, Lord. Open at your convenience.'"

It Stifles Your Praise

Praise rises up from our hearts when our eyes turn away from the mirror. The constant navel-gazing of self-examination, driven by a need for orthodoxy, leaves no energy for exuberant praise to the King of kings. In fact, *exuberant* becomes a questionable adjective. "We don't want to go overboard about this!" When "Everything in Moderation" becomes our motto, our praise will always be moderate. Nice, safe, moderate, and totally uninspired. But when it comes to expressing one's faith, Jesus doesn't applaud moderation. He condemned it in Simon and applauded the extravagance of the woman. She let it all out, and Jesus declared her forgiven because of it.

It Heightens Your Tendency to Impugn Motives

Overt expressions of passion for God are awfully intimidating to someone who doesn't allow themselves that luxury. They can seem overbearing or theatrical. They are quickly labeled as "show boating" or "putting your religion on your sleeve." And this often leads to mentally discrediting the one who's pushed our buttons and stretched our comfort zones.

For instance, if the raising of hands in praise isn't something you were "raised with," it probably makes you a tad uncomfortable when someone does so in your presence. I know I've felt that way. I've found myself unconsciously listing all the wrong motives that could be behind their hand raising and all the reasons why they needn't do it at all! Instead of looking at that very biblical expression of honor to the Lord in an objective way, I allowed my own fears and insecurities to blind me. Maybe that's what Simon felt. Maybe he just wanted to sidle up to the woman with the perfume and say, "Hey, you. Do you know what you're doing to the grading curve in this class? You're making all the rest of look like we don't care!"

It Closes You Off to New Experiences

By dismissing others' expressions of faith as "too much," the victim of Simonosis assumes their motive is something other than a genuine love for Christ and further disables himself from experiencing that kind of glorious abandon and release. If only Simon could have let go. If only he could have expressed the love for God trapped within him. Maybe he would have broken his own alabaster jar. Maybe he would have let his tears fall. But Simon's logical, emotionless approach to faith wouldn't allow it. "Why, how silly I would look on my knees."

Poor Simon. His shoes were just too tight to allow him to dance.

And he wasn't alone. He was a product of an environment that fostered a legalistic and passionless approach to faith. Yet Jesus didn't cut him much slack. Instead, he sought to jar Simon out of his complacency and mediocrity. Jesus challenged Simon to examine himself as he looked at this demonstrative, showy, expressive woman. He openly suggested that Simon may not realize how much he had to be thankful for. More than that, Simon was more concerned about this woman's actions than he was about his own inaction. As Jesus put it,

> *I came into your house. You did not give me any water for my feet, but she wet my feet with her tears and wiped them with her hair. You did not give me a kiss, but this woman, from the time I entered, has not stopped kissing my feet. You did not put oil on my head, but she has poured perfume on my feet. Therefore, I tell you, her many sins have been forgiven—for she loved much. But he who has been forgiven little loves little.* (Luke 7:44–47)

✦ The Dance of Celebration

So how could Simon change? What would be the Great Physician's prescription for the spiritual rigor mortis that had seized his soul? What would he recommend to those of us who suffer from a touch of Simonosis every now and then? I believe it might be a little two-step called the dance of celebration that goes like this:

Step #1: Accept Christ as Your Personal Savior

Before you start protesting that you gave your life to Jesus a long time ago, let me assure you that I accept your testimony. But could it be that you need to reaffirm the fact that Jesus is your Savior, that you are saved by *his* work, not yours. Like Martha, whom we discussed in the previous chapter, Simon felt that his relationship with God was based squarely on his performance appraisal. If he did everything just right, he'd get an A and go straight to the head of the class. That kind of pressure causes what some athletes refer to as *performance anxiety.*

But when we admit that salvation is far beyond our ability to attain and that we cannot earn it through right actions or right words, the pressure is released. It's like someone turned the valve and let the steam out. Exuberant praise can only be released when we come to Christ and say, "I'm completely, totally saved—and you're the one who did it."

The Hebrew writer helped his Jewish brethren see the glory in this truth:

> *You have not come to a mountain that can be touched and that is burning with fire. . . . But you have come to Mount Zion, to the heavenly Jerusalem . . . to Jesus the mediator of a new covenant, and to the sprinkled blood that speaks a better word than the blood of Abel.* (Hebrews 12:18, 22, 24)

The writer seems to say, "You think it was neat to stand at the bottom of Mount Sinai with Moses and see the thunder and the fire and the lightening? That ain't nothing; follow me!" He takes them through a glorious vision to the very center of the throne room of God and then points to the most important part of all—the blood of Christ that *"speaks a better word than the blood of Abel."*

But what does the blood of Abel say? Remembering the story of Cain's anger and Abel's murder, I think I can hear what his blood was saying—*Revenge! Payback!* "The blood of your brother cries out from the ground and says, 'Somebody go out there and avenge me.'"

Indeed, in ancient Israel if someone killed your brother, you would have had the right to kill them. You would have been called the "blood avenger." But in the new vision, it is Jesus' blood that is dripping off the altar. And can you hear what it is saying? It speaks a better word—*Enough, enough! No more sacrifice; no more!* Jesus' blood said, "Enough." You need not pay another debt; you need not take another life. Enough.

And we must listen and accept its words. His sacrifice on the cross is enough for eternity.

Step #2: Express Your Thanksgiving in Celebration

Having admitted that we are saved by Christ's blood and not our sweat, celebration must follow. But herein lies another challenge. Guilt and fear are without question powerful motivators. When they crack the whip, we jump. These insidious taunters know how to make us toe the line and stick to the rules. But they aren't very good at teaching us to dance. In fact, trying to celebrate your faith while being driven by guilt and fear is like trying to dance in a straight jacket. You may take a few painful steps, but you sure won't have any fun. Getting past the barriers that fear and guilt erect requires a concerted decision to celebrate. It necessitates a conscious choice to ignore the protestations of that critical voice in your head that never wants to risk being outlandish or extreme. It demands that you release control of your very body to the Spirit of God and allow yourself to become "a living sacrifice." It means saying "Hallelujah" right out loud.

✦

Guilt and fear
are powerful
motivators.
When they
crack the whip,
we jump.

✦

Admittedly, expressing feelings certainly comes easier for some folks than for others. But excuses like, "That's just not my nature," sound pretty pale when you hear Jesus say, "She loved much." And those same folks who claim that they just aren't demonstrative types can sure loosen their collars when their favorite team is in the Super Bowl or when they sink a twenty-five foot putt! No, our problem is more related to our willingness to stretch our comfort zones than our ability to express excitement.

But others suggest that our educated and cultured churches don't make the best forums for ecstatic praise. I would have to agree that some worship services are more conducive to slumber than celebration. But is there ever a really convenient time to break open that alabaster box? Why not just start making a practice of doing it weekly wherever you are. When you gather to praise God in worship, let your voice ring out in the singing. Try dropping to your knees to pray or maybe raising your hands in praise. Allow "Praise the Lord!" to become a regular part of your vocabulary outside the church building.

And don't overlook the many nonverbal ways of extravagantly expressing and celebrating your faith. Just as the woman gave a sacrifice in celebration, we, too, can pour out our time and talents in praise to God. Surprise a friend with a lengthy note of encouragement. Stop by to see an elderly saint, and stay for more than ten minutes. Write a check for an amount above and beyond what you think you can to your church treasury or favorite ministry. Whatever form of expression you choose will probably be uncomfortable at first, but go ahead and be extravagant, outlandish, and demonstrative. Pour out perfume. If it comes from a heart filled with gratitude, the smell of your sacrifice will motivate and inspire others to let their praises ring out as well.

Finally, when timidity tries to slow you down . . . remember Simon and the woman. Which of those two do you want to resemble?

Who knows? Before long, you just may find yourself dancing before the Lord . . . and enjoying it!

Jesus left there and went to his hometown, accompanied by his disciples. When the Sabbath came, he began to teach in the synagogue, and many who heard him were amazed.

"Where did this man get these things?" they asked. "What's this wisdom that has been given him, that he even does miracles! Isn't this the carpenter? Isn't this Mary's son and the brother of James, Joseph, Judas and Simon? Aren't his sisters here with us?" And they took offense at him.

Jesus said to them, "Only in his hometown, among his relatives and in his own house is a prophet without honor." He could not do any miracles there, except lay his hands on a few sick people and heal them. And he was amazed at their lack of faith.

✦ Mark 6:1–6

Nazaritis — Coma of the Soul

"Too Bored to Bop"

Wake up, O sleeper,
rise from the dead,
and Christ will shine on you.
(Ephesians 5:14)

I only saw my dad fall asleep in church once. And it really wasn't church.

Every summer, for as long as I could remember, we spent a week in the mountains at a camp with a hundred junior high and high school students—Camp Tanda. My father, as one of the camp's directors, oversaw the kitchen crew, helped with cabin inspections, and sometimes led singing at the devotionals. The schedule for the week was filled with hiking and horseback riding, and each evening concluded with some of the older teens from the camp trying out their public speaking skills by giving a sermon. After that came campfire and then bedtime . . . at least for the campers. My father and the other directors would take turns on the "Midnight Patrol," an exercise aimed at keeping the boys from fishing frogs out of the nearby lake and tossing them into the girls' tents. Curfew offenders were made to carry large rocks on a "forced march" around the camp before being sent to bed. While this was effective at wearing out the teens, it was just as exhausting for the adults.

> ◆
>
> He would shake his head a bit, as if to clear away the interior cobwebs, and then fix his eyes on the speaker with a fiercely interested look.
>
> ◆

One Thursday, after a particularly busy Wednesday night patrol, my dad's behavior caught my eye during the evening devotional. He was sitting in his customary spot on the front row of the "church bowl," a makeshift amphitheater underneath an army-surplus tarp that served as our sanctuary. I don't recall which of the young men was speaking that night, but it was pretty clear that preaching was not among the gifts God had blessed him with. I can still remember the shock I felt when I saw my father starting to nod off. As a kid who had caught my share of paternal pinches for falling asleep in church, I could hardly control the desire to walk over and give him a good pinch. But it was too much fun just to watch.

The picture was familiar to anyone who's ever watched a sleepy listener trying to stay awake during a boring sermon: His eyes would close, as if he were concentrating on the last point the speaker had made. Then, ever so slowly, his head would begin to dip. Just before his chin would reach his chest, he'd catch himself and snap his head back up with enough force to make the old bench he sat on creak. He would shake his head a bit, as if to clear away the interior cobwebs, and then fix his eyes on the speaker with a fiercely interested look. But within seconds, the lids would start to shut and the whole cycle would begin again.

After several minutes of vain attempts at finding a posture that would keep him vertical, he began casually placing one hymnal after another in his lap. I couldn't believe it! He was resorting to the oldest trick in the book. He stacked five songbooks in his lap, and then put his head in his hands and propped his elbows on the stack. Within seconds he was sound asleep, propped up like a statue, sitting right there on the front row, big as life! Ordinarily, this would have been only mildly amusing, but on this particular night my father was scheduled to *lead the singing*. As the young speaker drew toward his conclusion, I panicked. What would happen? I could just see Dad getting startled by the end of the lesson and falling off the bench as all those hymnbooks cluncked to the floor.

Then, rather abruptly, the young speaker concluded his remarks by offering an invitation and asking my father to lead a hymn. This was it—certain disaster. But to my amazement, Dad popped up like he'd been waiting all night for this moment. With a swift move, he set the songbooks aside as he belted out the appropriate song in perfect pitch. Now *that* was impressive! Later when I relayed the story to my mother, she smiled and said, "Why goodness, Jefferson. Your father's only been preaching for forty years. He could have done that in his sleep."

Her comment has stuck with me. I've reflected on it often, as I've spent my own share of sleepy hours on a church pew. But staying physically awake was often less challenging than staying mentally and spiritually awake. Growing up in a preacher's family meant attending every prayer meeting or revival series that came through town. By the time I was six, I'd heard enough gospel preaching to save five third-world countries. I knew the books of the Bible, the plan of salvation, and the second and third verses of most of the hymns in the book. As I grew, that "been there, done that" attitude only intensified. The church services were as predictable as sunrise, and my own spiritual life was just as routine. So, as a young adult, dancing with God was the furthest thing from my mind when someone mentioned worship.

Patterns of behavior that are familiar are comforting. That's why folks get really pushed out of shape when someone tinkers with the order of worship at their church. Yet there's more to "sleepy faith" than falling into a worship rut. Religion that becomes routine leaves the participants sleepwalking through their faith life with half-lidded spiritual eyes. Scripture, inspired by the Spirit to pierce their hearts, ends up bouncing off their sleepy souls amid thoughts of, "Boy, my cousin Ed ought to read that verse. He really needs it." Joy and exuberance are replaced with a soul-numbing lethargy; these sleepwalkers don't get too excited about anything, for they've seen it all before . . . twice. And effectively sharing their faith is hard to do while trying to swallow yet another yawn.

For a time I was convinced that this was a twentieth-century disease, born of too much high tech and not enough human touch. So I was both consoled and encouraged to find that the first case of being bored with Christ is recorded right in the pages of Mark's gospel. The story can give us some clues about how to overcome the spiritually comatose state I call *Nazaritis.*

✦ Nazaritis

It all began when Jesus took a trip back to Nazareth . . . *"Jesus left there and went to his hometown, accompanied by his disciples. When the Sabbath came, he began to teach in the synagogue, and many who heard him were amazed"* (Mark 6:1–2).

For the first twenty-eight years of his human life, Jesus had walked the dusty streets of this second-rate Jewish town. Nazareth wasn't known for being a hot spot on the trade route between Jerusalem and the north—more like a watering hole. Its neighboring cities looked on it with disdain, and saying "I'm from Nazareth" was as likely to earn you a laugh as anything else. But in the divine wisdom of God the Father, that's where he chose to have the Savior grow up. For twenty-eight years he played in those streets, shopped in that marketplace, and worshiped in that synagogue. And now, after going off to Galilee and becoming a famous rabbi, he was back for a visit. I can only imagine the synagogue ruler's pride as he introduced Jesus. "We have a treat this Sabbath. A young man from our own congregation is back with us today. And he's going to teach the morning lesson." What was he thinking as he handed the scroll to Jesus? "Hope this kid is good"? Whatever it was; he was in for a surprise.

✦

This was just the carpenter's kid from down the street—

a local yokel— and one with a questionable past at that.

✦

Mark records that as Jesus spoke, the people were "amazed" at his teaching. This is the same word Mark used to describe people's reaction to a miracle. It must have been some sermon. The synagogue would never be the same after this guest speaker. (And by the way, can you imagine the poor fellow's task the following Sabbath? How would you like to preach the Sunday after Christ spoke!) But oddly enough, the mood somehow shifted. Listen to their comments: *"'Where did this man get these things?' they asked. 'What's this wisdom that has been given him, that he even does miracles! Isn't this the carpenter? Isn't this Mary's son and the brother of James, Joseph, Judas and Simon? Aren't his sisters here with us?' And they took offense at him"* (Mark 6:2–4).

It's almost as though they had been caught up in his words at first, but then were overtaken by their own cynicism. After all, this wasn't some spiritual leader from the big city of Jerusalem. This was just the carpenter's kid from down the street—a local yokel—and one with a questionable past at that. *"Isn't this Mary's son?"*

Before you come down too hard on the folks from Nazareth, remember—this was a small town, and rumors die hard in small towns. Some of the people hearing Jesus that day were probably the ones who met his family when they moved in . . .

"I remember the day like it was yesterday. Fine looking young couple came riding into town on a donkey. She couldn't have been much more than seventeen, but he'd seen a few more Sabbaths than that, I'd wager. He said his name was Joseph, a woodworker by trade. I told him there was always room in town for a good carpenter. Wife's name was Mary, he says. 'And what about that cute little tyke you got on your shoulders? What's his name?' I asked. 'Jesus,' he says. 'Fine boy,' I told them; ' 'bout two years old, I'd say?' The lady nodded and said he'd just turned two that month. 'Well, happy birthday,' I says. Then I says, 'How long you folks been married?' And that's when they both got quiet. 'Two years,' he finally says. Well, I didn't just fall off the cheese wagon yesterday, if you catch my meaning. I just went on ahead like nothing was doing. Chatted another minute or two, and they was on their way. 'Poor kids, got a rough start of it,' I said to myself. 'Probably trying to get a clean start here.' Well, I was never one given to gossip, so I only told a few of my *closest* friends about it and . . ."

> ✦
>
> Boredom with Christ is the one thing that will disable him from accomplishing great things in our lives.
>
> ✦

The townspeople probably had more than a bit of resentment and memory in their eyes as they began to *"take offense."* They knew Jesus far too well to hear what he was saying. What could he possibly have to tell them? They had watched him grow up, and his siblings were still part of the synagogue. No telling what stories the townspeople had on them! So Jesus left Nazareth without fanfare, and his parting comments have become a well-known proverb: " *'Only in his hometown, among his relatives and in his own house is a prophet without honor.' He could not do any miracles there, except lay his hands on a few sick people and heal them. And he was amazed at their lack of faith"* (Mark 6:4–6).

Those last two sentences may be the most heartbreaking: *"He could not do any miracles there."* Why not? I used to attribute it to Jesus somehow, as though his resentment at their response prompted him to withhold his miraculous powers. But not only is that explanation inconsistent with the nature of the Lord, it isn't what the text points us toward. Mark tells us that he could only *"lay his hands on a few sick people."* Jesus was willing, as always, to heal anyone who would let him, but the Nazarenes' faith didn't let him. They literally didn't let him lay his hands on the truly sick in the town. They were so deceived by the familiarity-induced coma they had fallen into that they didn't see the powerful cures Jesus offered. And that amazed the Lord.

Now there's a pair of twin ironies for you: the same folks who had trusted him with their broken stools and cracked wagon wheels when he was working in his father's carpentry shop wouldn't trust him with a sick child or ailing parent when he had all the powers of heaven to banish illness. The commonplace blinded them to the supernatural.

But to top that, the same Lord who created heaven and earth is amazed, not by the breadth and depth of this awesome universe, but by the shallowness of the humans who inhabit it. It must take quite a bit to amaze the one who invented the concept of amazement!

And how often do we amaze him? How many mornings do we greet God with the same blasé spirit that the Nazarenes greeted Jesus? Boredom with Christ is the one thing that will disable him from accomplishing great things in our lives. For when we take him for granted, when we pigeonhole him as someone whose number we've got down, we are banishing the sense of the wonder that true faith always creates.

Here's a brief checklist from the Nazaritis symptom list to see if you may be suffering from a touch of this coma-inducing germ. Check off the statements that describe you:

❏ I am seldom touched by the communion and remembrance of Christ's sacrifice.

❏ It's been ages since I shed a tear over sin in my life.

❏ I switch off mentally as soon as I realize that the text for the preacher's sermon is one I've read before.

❏ I've been a Christian so long, I feel there isn't much more of significance that I need to learn.

❏ I am often resistant to hearing the criticism of someone younger in the faith, convinced that they have little to teach me.

❏ I can't remember the last time I was so overjoyed by the truth of my salvation that I shouted out loud.

❏ I'm often bored in prayer services.

If you checked one or two of the above, you may be in the early stages of Nazaritis. The rest of this chapter will offer some things that could be helpful. If you checked three to six statements, you've almost certainly been infected and may already be comatose. You should definitely keep reading. And if you checked all seven . . . well, that's a moot point. Those who are that far gone have probably quit reading this chapter already, as they don't think there's anything they can learn here anyway.

So how do you get the wonder back? How do you jump up and dance when you feel more like lying down for a nap? How do you put the amazing back in "Amazing Grace" when you've sung it all your life?

✦ A Spiritual Wake-up Call

We *can* awaken from the coma of Nazaritis, but only if we follow the prescription of the Great Physician. His directive closely corresponds to what were possibly some of the first instructions we ever received.

Do you remember how your parents taught you to cross the street? If they read from the same manual as mine, they chanted the same three words: "Stop, look, and listen." Let's allow these instructions to guide us once more.

Stop

Stop the routine of your religious life. Like the lulling clickity-clack of a rolling train, the rhythm of singing the same songs, praying the same prayers, and reading the same texts can bring sleepy stasis rather than spiritual growth. And when sameness has bred numbness, then a pause in the program is essential. Stop the train. Take a break. Pause in silence. Let God have a moment of your undivided attention.

The prophet Isaiah scolded Israel for her unwillingness to wait in quietness upon God:

> *This is what the Sovereign Lord, the Holy One of Israel, says:*
> *"In repentance and rest is your salvation,*
> *in quietness and trust is your strength,*
> *but you would have none of it.*
> *You said, 'No, we will flee on horses.'*
> *Therefore you will flee!*
> *You said, 'We will ride off on swift horses.'*
> *Therefore your pursuers will be swift!"*
> (Isaiah 30:15–16)

Like them, we are always ready to ride off on our horses and charge into the speedy tide of our lives without even a pause to wait upon our Captain. We must stop the action long enough to get a fresh perspective and renew our focus on God.

Like most steps in spiritual growth, this sounds much easier than it is. An accustomed routine is like a safety net into which we fall each day. Whether it is how we greet our spouse each morning or the radio station we listen to on the way to work, old habits are hard to break. But allow me to assure you that the rewards for changing the routine are many. My own experience with a broken radio convinced me.

It was a year or so ago that my car radio blew a fuse. As an "all-news" junky, I was driven to distraction at the thought of missing my fifteen-minute dose of the world's woes each morning. But just the first few days proved invaluable.

After instinctively reaching for the knob when I started the car, I resigned myself to the silence. And guess what . . . I had time to think. Oh, at first it was mainly about when and how I could get the radio repaired. But soon I realized that this little change in my routine was jarring something loose in my head. It allowed me to quietly prioritize my morning and give thanks for the new start each day provided. It helped me focus my thoughts on who I was called to be and what God was calling me to do at that moment. And most of all, it underlined the rush and fury with which I had grown accustomed to beginning my days. I actually started looking forward to the quiet moments before the roar of the workday commenced.

Had it not been for that faulty receiver making me stop in my tracks, I don't know if I would ever have discovered those wonderful truths. There is power in just stopping the routine. Do something you don't normally do. Read an author you haven't explored. Buy a CD of a Christian artist you don't normally listen to. Or just turn off your radio on the way to work and be jarred by the quiet. Soon you'll be driven to the second step.

Look

Look around you with fresh eyes of faith. Have you noticed how easy it is to stop really seeing your surroundings because they are so familiar? A behavioral scientist proved this in a remarkable way. To a group of college-age volunteers he rapidly showed twelve playing cards, exposing each one for only a split second. He asked them to record what cards they saw, and every member of the test group gave the same list. Again he exposed the cards, extending the amount of time they had to look at each one. Still their lists remained the same. After several more exposures, he asked if any of the cards were out of the ordinary. None could say they were. He then showed them each card for a full two seconds. Only at that point did they notice that among the cards they had been shown were a *black* heart and a *red* spade.

Our minds, as astounding as they are, quickly begin to disregard a static environment, assuming it to be the same as it has always been. Subtle changes often go unnoticed because we aren't truly "looking" at them. Consider what this can mean in the spiritual realm, and you will be brought back to Jesus' words to the Pharisees.

✦

In them is fulfilled the prophecy of Isaiah: "You will be ever hearing but never understanding; you will be ever seeing but never perceiving. For this people's heart has become calloused; they hardly hear with their ears, and they have closed their eyes. Otherwise they might see with their eyes, hear with their ears, understand with their hearts and turn, and I would heal them. (Matthew 13:14–15)

Have you noticed how easy it is to stop really seeing your surroundings because they are so familiar?

✦

A world of wonder awaits the believer who, having stopped the flood of life, will look around himself with open eyes. Look afresh at the communion, and you will see a moving and marvelous meal of love offered by the God whose banquet table stretches for eternity. Gaze anew at your family and your home, and you will see a cornucopia of blessings that God has poured into your life. Look with open eyes of the heart at your past, and you will see the outline of God's hand holding back harm and guiding your path.

But you must look with the eyes of a child. Open your heart's eyes to the wonder of seeing and hearing a world of love and joy so marvelous that you may be lead to tears.

If you question the fact that all that wonder could be lying unseen right under your nose, think again. It happens all the time. When a young friend from Kansas came to spend a week with us one summer, the first thing on his agenda was to see the ocean. We dropped his bags in our guest room and piled into the car for the brief ride to the beach. Having been blessed the last twenty years of my life to live within ten minutes of the Pacific, I knew a picturesque spot not three miles from our house and was even fortunate enough to get a good parking spot. This area of the coast is framed by a bluff with carved-out steps that descend to the sand. From the parking lot, you can't actually see the ocean. You must first walk over a small rise and turn a corner. Then suddenly, the massive Pacific is stretched out in front of you.

Ryan ran ahead of me to the corner and then froze in his tracks. His jaw fell slack, and his eyes widened in amazement.

Now this part of the beach wasn't normally busy, and I thought he must be staring at some nude bathers or maybe someone modeling a string bikini. I was already thinking of other spots where we might go when I reached the corner, but there wasn't a soul on the sand.

"What is it?" I asked.

"Look. Can you believe it?"

"What?" I responded, still not catching on.

"It's so . . . big."

It hit me that all he was gaping at was the ocean. "Of course it's big," I mentally quipped. "What did you expect? It's got to reach all the way to Japan!"

"It's just so big!" he moaned again. "Isn't it amazing? And you get to live right by it. That must be cool."

Only then did I begin to look at that huge expanse of water through my young friend's amazed eyes. And then I began to see it, too, and feel it . . . *wonder*.

"Can we go down and touch it?"

"Sure, why not." And before you knew it, there we were, shoes in hand and pants rolled up to our knees, wading in that chilling water . . . and being amazed.

"If I lived here," he said as we were putting on our shoes to head back to the car, "I'd come here once every day just to look at this." I only nodded. I couldn't bring myself to tell him that although I lived only minutes from it, I had not touched that water in nearly a year. I just hadn't been looking with open eyes.

Listen

Listen for the voice of God in every day. He speaks volumes to those who will take the time to listen. And though the words may be familiar, by meditating on his message, they become fresh again. And as they call you, let your heart follow where they lead.

Listen for the call of God to pain and tears. Don't run from them, but accept and embrace them. They lead us to need him more.

Listen for the call of God to service and sacrifice. Through giving and sharing we find more life than we ever knew we had.

Listen to the call of God to celebrate and praise. Release your feelings to revel in the ecstasy they offer. No pleasure on earth is as sweet or holy.

Listen to the call of God to change and grow. When new challenges arise and tougher

✦

Listen for the call of God to pain and tears. Don't run from them, but accept and embrace them.

✦

tests of faith loom in your path, accept them with the assurance that God is molding you more into his likeness and shaping you for joys yet unseen.

One final word of caution is needed. Renewing your spirit and reviving from the coma of Nazaritis *once* will not cure you for life. Most believers have to stop, look, and listen on a daily basis to keep from slipping back into that sleepy world of colorless faith.

I've heard some wonder out loud whether God would give them a second chance if, after knowing the joy of dancing with him, they fell asleep once again. For them, the Nazarene has good news. The incident in Mark 6, which we've studied in this chapter, was not the first time Jesus had gone back to Nazareth. Luke records what must have been an earlier return visit in which the people of the town actually tried to throw Jesus off a cliff! (Luke 4:29). Yet to that ungrateful and spiritually comatose city, he returned. He came back to offer them another chance.

Why?

Because that's the kind of Savior he is—he's the Lord of Second Chances, the Prince of Patience. And that's why you're always invited to come "stand amazed in the presence of Jesus, the *Nazarene.*"

SO David went down and brought up the ark of God from the house of Obed-Edom to the City of David with rejoicing. When those who were carrying the ark of the Lord had taken six steps, he sacrificed a bull and a fattened calf. David, wearing a linen ephod, danced before the Lord with all his might, while he and the entire house of Israel brought up the ark of the Lord with shouts and the sound of trumpets.

As the ark of the Lord was entering the City of David, Michal daughter of Saul watched from a window. And when she saw King David leaping and dancing before the Lord, she despised him in her heart.

✦ 2 Samuel 6:12–16

Michalepsy – The Critic's Blindness

"What, me? Do that?"

From the moment he came through the door, he could tell she was mad. She had that sour look on her face that could only be one of two things: indigestion or irritation. And something told him it was the latter.

"Don't spoil today," he must have thought. This has been such a great day—one for the record books. The ark of God was back in Jerusalem at last. The symbol of God's power and presence had been kept in exile for nearly twenty years, and now it was finally in its proper place. It had taken three months for him to get it to the city, and the trip had cost one man his life. The celebration as it came through the gates had been exhilarating.

But he had a pretty good notion that she wasn't thinking about any of that just now. No, she was definitely not in a partying mood. Something was most certainly wrong. At least he didn't have to wait long to find out what the problem was. None of this, "How was your day, dear?" prattle for her. She cut straight to the chase and let him have it. *"How the king of Israel has distinguished himself today, disrobing in the sight of the slave girls of his servants as any vulgar fellow would!"* (2 Samuel 6:20).

With those words, Michal, the wife of King David, sealed her fate and provided generations with a classic example of misplaced judgment and wrong-headed thinking. Her judgmental attitude would cost her dearly, so it's fitting that we learn from her loss. The same attitudes that kept her from joining her husband in celebrating God's blessings two millennia ago are keeping thousands from that same enjoyment today. In fact, *Michalepsy* may be more common than any of the other diseases of the spirit we've addressed. It strikes believers of all ages, cutting off any hope of dancing with God in unfettered praise.

If you've ever held back from expressing your faith in God for fear that someone might criticize . . . If you have ever looked with envy at exuberant Christians and wondered why they had what you didn't . . . If you have ever sat in a worship service and felt somehow cheated because you didn't feel free to express the exaltation you saw those around you expressing . . . If you haven't dared to dance with God because of the eyebrows you might raise . . . welcome to the Michalepsy ward. To understand her disease, we must answer two questions: What was the story behind the dance, and why was David dancing?

✦ The Ark Comes Home

It had been a long road for David. God had brought him all the way from the sheep pen to the palace. Although the crown was on his head and the scepter in his hand, the ark of the covenant had

142

not joined him within the walls of Jerusalem. The center of Hebrew government and the center of Hebrew religious life could not be united until the ark was returned to Jerusalem. That amazing box carried not just relics of Jewish history but the presence of the Lord God as well. It had accompanied the Israelites in defeat of their enemies and was instrumental in God's parting of the Jordan River. It had led Israel in the wilderness and gone before them into the Promised Land. It had even been used to punish the Israelites. In a time of idolatry and disobedience, God had allowed the Philistines to take the ark. But they got more trouble than they had bargained for, and it was soon returned. Then it had been parked at the house of Abinadab in the city of Baalah for two decades. When the palace was finally built in Jerusalem, the time had seemed right to bring up the ark.

♦

No, she was definitely not in a partying mood. Something was most certainly wrong.

♦

The first time David went to retrieve it, he'd taken thirty thousand men and charged up to get the ark like a general storming a city. They hastily loaded it onto a brand-new cart and, thoughtlessly ignoring God's instructions on how the ark was to be moved, tried hauling it behind a pair of oxen. When the oxen stumbled and the ark began to slide off the cart, Uzzah, one of the sons of Abinadab, reached out to steady it and was struck dead by God on the spot.

It's fair to note that the judgment brought on Uzzah may seem harsh in our eyes. But be sure that this man knew what he was doing. Since he had been a boy on his father Abinadab's knee, he had been taught about the ark. When the wonderful thing came to reside in their backyard, he must have known that it was not to be touched on pain of death (Numbers 4:14–15). Surely he had heard the stories of what happened in Beth Shemesh. When the ark had first been sent there by the Philistines, seventy men had died when they tried to get a peek inside. He knew that the Lord never intended for the ark to be moved on an ox cart. It had loops built into its sides for the wooden poles designed to carry it. God had decreed that the ark of his presence would be borne by his people, not dragged along behind a pair of animals.

Nevertheless, the incident shocked the whole company. The second book of Samuel records David's reactions: *"Then David was angry because the Lord's wrath had broken out against Uzzah, and to this day that place is called Perez Uzzah. David was afraid of the Lord that day and said, 'How can the ark of the Lord ever come to me?'"* (2 Samuel 6:8–9).

It must have been a long, quiet march back to Jerusalem—the dejected and angry king, followed by the soldiers carrying the body of Uzzah. David waited three months before going back to try again.

But this time there was no ox cart. He ordered that the ark be carried by the Levites. And this would be no frantic rush to bring a trophy home. David assembled the men to carry it with great reverence. No one was joking as they shouldered the poles and lifted the ark. They all remembered Uzzah. When everyone was in place, they began to move. And when the group had walked six steps, David stopped the whole parade, made an offering, and thanked God for returning his favor to them. So humbled and thankful was David that he stripped down to just his linen ephod, the simple tunic that the servant of a priest would wear.

✦ David's Dance

Without his kingly robe and crown, David danced *"with all his might before the Lord."* Years of longing and waiting had finally come to an end. God had blessed his people, and the king did not contain his joy. On the contrary, he commanded others to join with him. First Chronicles 15:16 says he appointed singers and musicians to accompany the celebration as they entered Jerusalem. He was determined that everyone would know of this wonderful

144

moment. The streets must have been filled with cheering crowds as the king danced and praised his way into the city.

And how could he dance with such gusto? He had his gaze firmly set on the power and mercy of God. He had seen the Lord's power and judgment when he struck down Uzzah. He had looked into the dead man's face and cursed his own thoughtlessness. But he had also seen the gracious hand of God's mercy when he had allowed them to once more carry the sacred chest. In short, he couldn't help but celebrate.

And neither can anyone who looks with honesty at the majesty of God. When I think of his love and care for me, I, too, am moved to forget my status or social graces and just jump up and shout in delight.

✦ Michalepsy

But sometimes, instead of dancing, I stumble into Michal's mistake: While David's eyes were on God, hers were on David. *"As the ark of the Lord was entering the City of David, Michal daughter of Saul watched from a window. And when she saw King David leaping and dancing before the Lord, she despised him in her heart"* (2 Samuel 6:16).

What moved Michal to hate David? Some have suggested she was ruing the fact that her own father, Saul, had not been the one leading this triumphal entry. But her remarks to David about the incident give us a better clue to the source of her disgust. Take another look at her words. *"How the king of Israel has distinguished himself today, disrobing in the sight of the slave girls of his servants as any vulgar fellow would!"*

Michal was embarrassed. The blood had rushed to her cheeks while she stood on that balcony watching her husband. The graciousness of God and the power of his presence had been the furthest things from her mind as she leered at the scene. She had instead focused on what others must have been saying about David's action. She was more worried about what the servant girls thought than what the Lord had done. She allowed herself to disregard everything of importance and zoom in on David's choice of outfit for this historic occasion. In essence she was saying, "How could you act so . . . *blue collar!*"

I can see her pacing and fuming as she waited for him to finish all the celebrations and come home. Each minute she had to wait only added to her anger as she mulled over just how she would dress down her already undressed spouse. Her mind scrolled through the names of the people who saw him in the streets—people beneath her status. Just the thought of those slave girls giggling about how her husband looked in that slinky linen ephod was enough to wind her clock up tight. If you had tried to remind her that the return of the ark of the covenant was the real issue, I doubt you would have made much headway. No, this was about decorum and culture. This was about pride and position. This was about having to face the next meeting of the Jerusalem Ladies Auxiliary after they had all watched her hubby boogying in his royal underwear!

> ✦
>
> In essence she was saying, "How could you act so . . . *blue collar!*"
>
> ✦

This kind of angry judgment has silenced plenty of euphoric believers through the centuries. There's never been a short supply of uptight critics to scold Christians who sang too loud, raised their hands too high, or *amen*ed too often. Their smirks and quips are designed to keep the worship of God from becoming too brazen, too raucous, too *anything*. And they are with us today. Michal was just the first in a long line of "church police" who see it as their mission in life to insure that praising, if done at all, is done with refinement and propriety.

But David would not be cowed by her spite. His feelings were, if anything, embolded by her reaction. He not only stood up to her, he gave her what seems to be to be a long-overdue rebuke.

> *David said to Michal, "It was before the Lord, who chose me*
> *rather than your father or anyone from his house when he*
> *appointed me ruler over the Lord's people Israel—I will cele-*
> *brate before the Lord. I will become even more undignified*
> *than this, and I will be humiliated in my own eyes. But by*
> *these slave girls you spoke of, I will be held in honor."*
> (2 Samuel 6:21–22)

His first words pinpoint the issue: He was not dancing for her or anyone else on earth. He was celebrating with and for the Lord. To David, terms like *"humiliated"* and *"undignified"* were badges of honor, not shame. And the opinion of the slave girls that Michal seemed so worried about was never in question. David promises that they will honor him long after Michal is out of the picture. Which, it seems from the next verse, may not have been very long. *"And Michal daughter of Saul had no children to the day of her death."*

Whether by her husband's choice or God's decree, Michal was punished for her judgmental nature. Though it's tempting just to imagine how David's response might shut the mouths of some modern-day Michals we know, it is more important to consider how to avoid her sickness all together.

✦ Mind Your Own Praise

What Michal needed was a review of a basic principle of good dancing . . . and healthy praising: focus on God—not on everyone else. Her desire to regulate her husband's behavior could have been curbed if she had followed two simple rules drawn from David's response. They are well worth our noting.

Rule #1: Keep Your Eyes on Your Partner

Training the eyes of our heart on God will free our dancing in more ways than one. First, keeping your eyes solidly on your dance partner keeps you from being distracted by onlookers. Hebrews contains an image that illustrates this well.

The New Testament letter to the Hebrews is an epistle of encouragement. Written to Jewish believers who were trying to hang on to their newfound faith, it gives advice on maintaining your direction in the face of critical opposition. The famous metaphor of the Christian race found in the twelfth chapter contains a command that's critical to dancing with God: *"Therefore, since we are surrounded by such a great cloud of witnesses, let us throw off everything that hinders and the sin that so easily entangles, and let us run with perseverance the race marked out for us. Let us fix our eyes on Jesus, the author and perfecter of our faith"* (Hebrews 12:1–2).

The writer pictures a stadium filled with spectators watching us run the race of faith. The witnesses he refers to may be angels or saints from years gone by. Some imagine Moses and Joshua sitting next to Noah and Jacob munching popcorn and cheering us on from the stands. While their presence may be motivating, notice that the writer never tells us to look at the spectators. Quite the opposite. After commanding us to strip off anything that might hold us back from running freely toward God—a directive that strangely reminds one of David stripping down to his linen ephod—he tells us to *"fix our eyes on Jesus."*

While the crowd pictured in Hebrews 12 may be an encouraging one, the crowds that surround us on earth aren't always so. But whether our crowd cheers or boos us, we must keep our gaze locked on Christ's loving face. It makes sense. The fickle crowd can easily distract or dishearten. One minute they love you and the next they're calling for the coach to pull you from the game. Not so Jesus. He always pulls for you. His eyes are always filled with hope. Like the apostle Peter walking on the water, we'll not sink as long as our eyes are on him.

Second, maintaining a focus on God will take our praise to heights that nothing else can. I have heard it suggested that exuberant praise is a great witness to the nonbeliever. And though I can't agree more, I must never allow my focus to shift from praising God because he is great to praising God because it will attract or influence others. Not only would that corrupt the purity of my motive for praise, it would divert my attention from the source of my passion. What greater motive for praise is there than the great mercy of God? There's nothing more moving than looking into eyes that are filled with love.

As a minister, I've seen that truth proven up close. At most of the wedding ceremonies I've presided over there comes a point where the groom begins to get the nervous shakes. You can almost see him start thinking about who's sitting out there watching him or how uncomfortable his tux is. Soon, his fingers start to twitch and a little bead of sweat rolls from his temple to his collar. Now, if this hits about the time for him to say his vows, you've got trouble. No matter how intelligent and capable a guy this may be, chances are, if he doesn't get focused, he could end up like one groom who substituted the name of an old girlfriend for his bride's name when he said, "I Richard, take thee Janet . . . I mean Jamie!"

Through the years I've tried several methods of calming nervous grooms, but there's only one that's literally "fool" proof. I just say, "Will you repeat these words after me *as you look into the eyes of your bride.*" It never fails. When his eyes meet hers, all other thoughts flee. Like magic they are both transported to some other realm, and he speaks with the passionate inspiration that only love can give. That same inspiration is available to the believer who looks deeply into the eyes of a loving Lord. See his eyes on the cross. See his eyes at the tomb of Lazarus. See his eyes when forgiving the harlot. See his eyes looking at you. Lock your gaze on his, and your praise will surely soar to new heights.

Third, keeping our eyes on God will meter our praise better than any human judge. If I am earnestly channeling my praise straight to him, his overwhelming holiness and purity will keep my exuberance in balance. If I do begin to dance out of step with him, it will quickly be evident. His righteousness will leave no room for my impropriety. As John declares. *"God is light; in him there is no darkness at all."* If I look with commitment on his good-ness, I will have little trouble keeping my praise pure.

Rule #2: Keep Your Eyes Off Others

Spiritual freedom is a two-edged sword. It allows me to express my love for God in any form I choose, but it also allows others to express their love in ways I may not care for! As much as I believe that most conservative Christians need a healthy dose of freedom in Christ, I am often unsettled by what freedom can bring. I suppose that we are far enough along in this discourse for me to come clean on this issue: outlandish and overly expressive demonstrations of praise make me nervous. And folks whose praise seems designed to be seen by men more than by God always makes my stomach hurt. As I have said before, the conservative Christian background God blessed me with didn't include any raising of hands and only precious few *hallelujah*s. Though I know the folly of the notion, I daily wrestle with the belief that I can ascertain a person's sincer-ity by the style of their praise. If they come on too strong, a bell rings somewhere in the back office of my mind over a warning light that says "counterfeit!"

That's why this concept is so important for me. Jesus addresses the same problem in the sermon on the mount: *"Do not judge, or you too will be judged. For in the same way you judge others, you will be judged, and with the measure you use, it will be measured to you. Why do you look at the speck of sawdust in your brother's eye and pay no attention to the plank in your own eye?"* (Matthew 7:1–3).

A judgmental spirit may be motivated by at least two forces: spiritual covetousness or fear of what others will think.

First, if my eyes wander off of my Lord and onto the praise of others, I may find myself spiritually coveting that believer's gifts. It's disturbing enough that someone else seems to be experiencing a more transcendent joy in the Lord, but it becomes almost unbear-able if I have to watch them from the sidelines. My own limitations leave me feeling cheated and left out and wondering "Why don't I feel like they look?"

Those thoughts always remind me of a story a friend of mine tells about the last question a young lady asked him before being baptized. While standing in the baptistery with him awaiting the end of the hymn preceding the baptism, the young candidate asked, "What will it feel like when I receive the gift of the Holy Spirit?" My friend now had thirty seconds, maximum, to explain his understanding of the doctrine of the filling of the Holy Spirit. Remembering the nervousness he felt at his own baptism, he summed up his thoughts as best he could: "The Bible tells us that we are given the gift of the Holy Spirit when we commit our lives to God. I can't tell you what, if anything, you may feel; but the important thing to know is that God promises that his Spirit will live in you from this day forward." At that moment the hymn concluded and the curtain opened.

Still mulling over the quality of his impromptu answer, he took her confession of faith and tipped her back, immersing her in the water. The second her face was fully submerged, her body stiffened and her eyes popped open. The look on her face was a mixture of excitement and surprise. And all he could think was, "Hey, Lord! How come I didn't get that!" As he pulled her up from the water, she put her hand on the back of her head; only then did he realize what had happened. During their conversation he had moved toward one end of the baptistery, and when he had lowered her into the water, he had smacked the back of her head onto the baptistery steps!

◆

It's disturbing enough that someone else seems to be experiencing a more transcendent joy in the Lord, but it becomes almost unbearable if I have to watch them from the sidelines.

◆

God gives his gifts in the way he chooses. While I must never close the door of my heart to what God may wish to provide, I cannot spend my spiritual life trying to attain what someone else seems to have.

My job is not to analyze the faith expressions of other Christians. To do so requires that I stop praising and start prying, using my precious time to compare myself to others. No, my task is to focus on God and give him all glory, honor, and praise.

♦

You will never be able to satisfy all who would care to examine your spiritual performance.

♦

Second, a judgmental spirit can also be symptomatic of a faith whose worth is based on the estimations of others. Years of enslavement to the criticism of critical believers creates an unhealthy mind-set: "As they have done to me, so I must do to others." If checking the third eye of public opinion becomes second nature, turning one's judgment on others' praise seems like the only fair turn. That's why questions like, "What would Brother So-and-So think if he saw me doing this?" come so quickly to some minds. Unfortunately, legalism of this sort is a treadmill with no "off" switch, for you will never be able to satisfy all who would care to examine your spiritual performance. Knowing this, Paul wrote in his letter to the Corinthian church: *"I care very little if I am judged by you or by any human court; indeed, I do not even judge myself. My conscience is clear, but that does not make me innocent. It is the Lord who judges me"* (1 Corinthians 4:3–4).

That kind of freedom is not a claim that we are immune to all judgment, but a recognition that we are judged by God alone. He is the only audience that matters. His opinion is the only one we should constantly poll.

True, the Scriptures teach that we must take care never to use our freedom to purposefully harm another believer. To become so swept up in the dance that I forget to encourage and uplift my brothers and sisters is selfish and sinful. But lest any think their fellow believer's concerns should control what they do for the Lord, a review of Paul's advise on binding opinions is in order.

> *One man's faith allows him to eat everything, but another man, whose faith is weak, eats only vegetables. The man who eats everything must not look down on him who does not, and the man who does not eat everything must not condemn the man who does, for God has accepted him. Who are you to judge someone else's servant?* (Romans 14:2–4)

The last question Paul poses is the first one we should think of when the urge to judge is felt. "Who am I to criticize the gift of a fellow believer?" And rather than viewing this as a restriction, we should see it as a relief. What good news it is to know that I am neither the judge of others nor subject to the judgment of others. "God has accepted him." That's the sentence I need to write fifty times when my critical nature acts up. Do I really want to give Jehovah a lecture on what's appropriate in praising him?

So remember poor Michal, the sad star of this cautionary tale. And remember that even though her motives may have been noble, her words still cost her dearly. Keep your eyes on the One who deserves your attention, and keep your attention from the ones who don't need your scorn. You will be helping their dance by honoring the freedom that Jesus died to give them. And you'll be aiding your own dance by following another one of God's divine ballroom rules: You can't play the critic and dance with the King.

Michal's end should convince us that critizing the praise of others is not a dance that God will join us in.

Learning to
Dance
When It
HURTS

♦ SECTION THREE
3 Special Dances for
Painful Times

There are moments so wonderful that you want to hold them forever: the first time you cradle your newborn child in your arms, the first time you kiss the love of your life, and the first time you realize that Christ died for you.

There are moments so terrible that you want to avoid them forever: the last time you hug a loved one before she dies, the last time you beg for mercy and are denied, and the last time you promise yourself things will be different.

Because life is made up of both kinds of moments, these special dances must be studied. They deal with a nasty trio—sin, pain, and death. And they are learned in the crucible of heartbreak. Don't expect them to be pleasant or comfortable. Only know that they are necessary.

And that God is willing to dance them with you.

The teachers of the law and the Pharisees brought in a woman caught in adultery. They made her stand before the group and said to Jesus, "Teacher, this woman was caught in the act of adultery. In the Law Moses commanded us to stone such women. Now what do you say?" They were using this question as a trap, in order to have a basis for accusing him.

But Jesus bent down and started to write on the ground with his finger. When they kept on questioning him, he straightened up and said to them, "If any one of you is without sin, let him be the first to throw a stone at her." Again he stooped down and wrote on the ground.

At this, those who heard began to go away one at a time, the older ones first, until only Jesus was left, with the woman still standing there. Jesus straightened up and asked her, "Woman, where are they? Has no one condemned you?"

"No one, sir," she said.

"Then neither do I condemn you," Jesus declared. "Go now and leave your life of sin."

✦ John 8:3–11

11

Doing the Sinner's Tango

Beyond the Shame Game

Where had they been when they were discovered?

Had they been in a house? If they had been in the back bedroom, they might not have heard the intruders coming; when the curtain was torn aside, the look on their faces would have been worthy of a *Life* magazine cover photo.

Had the couple been in the country? If so, the rustling of the bushes might have tipped them off—but still, there would have been no time. Before you could say, "Surprise!" they would have had her by the arms and been gone.

Had they been at her place? Ah, now there's a picture for you. The observers could have been hiding in the alley across the road like Jewish FBI agents on a stakeout. When the man went in, the nervous glance over his shoulder would have tipped them off. But, then they would have waited until the couple had enough time to get . . . busy. When the signal was given, they would have stormed in, pointing fingers and hollering condemnation, then stormed out, dragging her in smug triumph while she pleaded and cried.

Now, where would they go?

As the angry procession hurried through the streets, an impromptu parade must have formed. You didn't have to be a Hebrew scholar to know what was about to happen—someone had been caught in the act, and a stoning was coming. Shopkeepers joined the march. Old ladies wagged their heads and fell in step. Children, seeing the growing procession, ran alongside. And when they turned the corner and the street began to slope upward, it dawned on the woman that they weren't heading for the council house or the city gate. In a moment of horror, she realized where they were taking her—the temple.

✦

How can you join with God in embracing joy when the last thing you want to do is look him in the eye?

✦

"Not the temple!" she must have thought "Of all the places on earth! God have mercy; not the temple!" The Mount of Jehovah. The House of Yahweh. The Holy Hill. The place where priests made sacrifices and the devoted came to pray. An odd thought flashed through her mind: "If I had known we were coming here, I would have dressed for the occasion." But the humor died as they passed a silversmith's shop and she caught sight of her reflection in a large tray—a bedraggled, half-naked woman being driven along by gray-bearded religious officials. She had only a sheet wrapped around her—they hadn't given her time to dress; her nakedness added to the humiliation that was their goal.

And then they were there: the outer temple court. With a final shove, they flung her to the ground at the feet of a man she didn't recognize. Instinctively, she covered her head and waited for the first stone to strike. "Make it quick, Lord," she prayed. Would it hurt? How long before she would be unconscious? Then one of her captors spoke: *"Teacher, this woman was caught in the act of adultery. In the Law Moses commanded us to stone such women. Now what do you say?"*

Heads turned and comments flew—*"Wicked sinner!"* . . . *"Harlot!"* . . . *"Shame on her!"* That's exactly what they wanted. It's what good society always wants when it sees sin—*shame*. Shame on the drug addict and the dope dealer. Shame on the thief and the burglar. Shame on the con man and the rapist. As a friend's grandmother used to say, *"Shame all over you!"*

So how are you supposed to dance when you've got shame all over you? How can you join with God in embracing joy when the last thing you want to do is look him in the eye?

There is a special dance for the times when we are caught in the act. It's not a tap dance around the truth or a sidestep that seeks to point the blame elsewhere. It's a dance of honesty and humility. And yes, it's a dance of shame. But not the shame you may think. We'll use this nameless woman from the sixth chapter of John's gospel to lead the way.

✦ Shame on the Sinner

"Shame on that woman!" Sin brings shame. We must begin there. God built that law into man's spiritual ecology: when we disobey his will, shame should follow. But our society is uncomfortable with that. We look for ways to dodge the bullet of shame. We rationalize our alternative lifestyles or claim victim status, crying that our parents pushed us too hard or that the beer bottle was too easy to reach. No such claims were made by this woman. She silently lay before Christ in all her shame.

And so should we. The path out of sin's pit begins with a recognition of our shame. It belongs to us—we must own it. Look at

David's description of his shame for Israel at a time when their disobedience had led to punishment from God: *"You have made us a reproach to our neighbors, the scorn and derision of those around us. You have made us a byword among the nations; the peoples shake their heads at us. My disgrace is before me all day long, and my face is covered with shame"* (Psalm 44:13–15).

While this may not conform to the popular concept of a healthy self-image, it is a healthy dose of reality. We have all experienced it: a hard, honest look at one's life brings shame to anyone who knows God's standards. Memories of bad choices and willful disobedience are never far from reach, for sin is a habit harder to break than breathing. While we dedicate ourselves to its destruction, we resign ourselves to the fact that it will not be totally destroyed until Jesus comes again. Yes, its power to condemn was crucified with Christ, but the shame that sin brings was not buried in the garden tomb. It is meant to warn us that we have wandered into sinking sand. It is meant to challenge us with the holiness of God's will. But it is not meant to be our constant companion and daily partner. And its power to keep us from dancing in celebration can only be broken when we look full into its scowling face. Recognition and confession of shame open the door to beginning again.

◆

"I've done something terrible, and I need to turn myself in."

◆

But if we avoid that look, if we refuse to accept shame for what it is, guilt will burrow down inside us like a tapeworm, eating away at the foundation of our souls. Shame swept under the emotional rug can become a hidden monster of guilt that swallows our sleep and peace all in one bite. Examples surround us, but the following story breaks my heart.

On a spring morning in 1989, the police department in Troy, New York, received a call from an elderly woman. A trembling voice said, "I've done something terrible, and I need to turn myself in." As the desk sergeant scribbled furiously, she confessed to mur-

162

dering a newborn infant, placing its body in a strong box, and burying it in her backyard . . . forty years ago. The policeman's natural scepticism matched his surprise. "Lady, are you serious?" After a moment's silence she replied, "I was young and single, and I didn't know what to do. Everyday since then, I've looked out my back window and felt so guilty. I just can't sleep anymore." Sure enough, when the investigators dug in the spot she showed them, they found a small metal box containing what appeared to be the skeleton of an infant.

Forty years. That's a long time to live under a suffocating cloud of guilt and shame. I can't help but imagine the days she spent weeding that backyard and trying not to stare at that spot of ground. Imagine the nights she spent wondering if she could ever outlive it, wondering if she would ever be worth anything again. The only way she could deal with the guilt was to face the shame. If she didn't, she certainly would never be able to dance again.

Facing shame isn't supposed to be pleasant. Shame hurts. Shame harms. Shame pressures. It is designed to work that way, for it is the godly sorrow that drives us to the foot of the cross. It is the look in the mirror that strips away our pretense of righteousness and reminds us that we are all sinners saved by grace. It is the admission of our need for a savior that prepares us to take his hand.

But there's more shame in this picture.

✦ Shame on the Accusers

As Jesus looked around the circle of sanctimonious wolves, he found a way to give them their share of the shame. He bent down and began to write on the ground. Much has been said about his writing in the sand, but the text doesn't give us a clue as to what he scribbled. Did he write out some of the Ten Commandments or simply the words "Judge not"? I've heard more than one preacher say that they're going to ask Jesus what he was writing when they get to heaven, but I'm convinced that when we get there, those kinds of questions won't be on our minds.

But we are told what the accusers were up to and what Jesus said to them. *"They were using this question as a trap, in order to have a basis for accusing him"* (John 8:6).

The intent of the Jews was to catch Christ in controversy. They had him trapped between two unsavory choices. A merciful response on his part would give them all the ammunition they needed to tar his reputation and challenge his authority. But a harsh and rigid reply would surely lose him points with the crowd and put him in the same "catch 'em and stone 'em" league as all the other coldly pious religious leaders. But Christ had another agenda in mind. He chose not to answer their question at all but to ask his own instead. And there was shame in his words: *"If any one of you is without sin, let him be the first to throw a stone at her."*

He needn't have gone any further than the first eight words. No one in that circle could comply with his condition. No one in the circle of the earth can either, save the Savior himself. Even the Pharisees were wise enough to recognize this. *"At this, those who heard began to go away one at a time, the older ones first, until only Jesus was left, with the woman still standing there"* (John 8:9).

But the question wasn't designed to get a volunteer. It was meant to uncover the shame of those who had come to give shame to the woman. Their interest was not justice or truth. They simply wanted to see this woman squirm—and Jesus with her. They were much like many conservative Christians of our day—ever ready to review and discuss the sins of the heathen crowd outside the church doors. With belittling language and spiteful tones, shame is hurled by the handfuls—at gang-bangers, gays, and gun-running crack dealers. And the intent is often the same as the Jews who surrounded the woman: *"We want you to feel the shame! We want to make sure that you know, we know."*

A young Christian lady who had given birth out of wedlock recalled being told that she could not return to services at her church without first going before the whole congregation and confessing her sin. She didn't question the importance of confession and prayer, but the perceived motive angered her. "It was like they all wanted to see me crawl."

Maybe it would have been appropriate for her to have carried a rock with her when she walked down the church aisle. One Christian worker I know keeps one on his desk, labeled "The first stone." On occasion he'll offer it to someone who seems bent on blaming and shaming a fellow believer. But so far, no one has taken the rock. Its voice is too clear: "Shame on your judgmental attitudes. Shame on pointed fingers and 'better than you' looks. Shame on religious snobbery and theological one-upmanship that pits my tradition against yours. Shame on you for trying to throw shame on someone else!"

But be careful. Jesus' response was not a petty tit-for-tat. He was not suggesting that we join in the "Battle of the Blame." Our natural defense systems will prompt us to respond to the "shamers" of the world in kind. We want to fight fire with fire and accusation with accusation. Soon, and without realizing it, we are lured into the same shameful practice as our accusers, pointing our fingers at them as they point theirs at us, shouting, "You're shameful too!" And so they may be. But casting blame and pronouncing shame isn't my job. In fact, when I do, I rob Satan of his number-one job.

> *The great dragon was hurled down. . . . Then I heard a loud voice in heaven say: "Now have come the salvation and the power and the kingdom of our God, and the authority of his Christ. For the accuser of our brothers, who accuses them before our God day and night, has been hurled down.* (Revelation 12:9–10)

Satan is busy twenty-four hours a day, accusing God's people and challenging our right to God's mercy. You can't dance with God while trying to help Satan do his job. Accepting the shame of our own sin is one thing. Highlighting the shame of my brother's is another. His shame and mine can be taken away only when we

165

acknowledge our sin and offer it to the one who bore the greatest shame of all.

✦ Shame on Jesus

The final shame is on Christ himself. The one without sin, the one who had every right to throw a stone, took the shame instead. Even as he took the attention off of the accused woman, he took her shame on himself. The moving words of Isaiah paint the picture well:

> *Surely he took up our infirmities*
> *and carried our sorrows,*
> *yet we considered him stricken by God,*
> *smitten by him, and afflicted.*
> *But he was pierced for our transgressions,*
> *he was crushed for our iniquities;*
> *the punishment that brought us peace was upon him,*
> *and by his wounds we are healed.*
>
> (Isaiah 53:4–5)

Shame from sin doesn't just evaporate. It can't be expelled by wishing it away. In the court of God's will, someone must answer for the crime. Jesus was willing and able to be that someone. He allows me the chance to dance again, even after I sin—if I will give him my shame. Having faced and acknowledged my culpability, I hold out my guilt, which he graciously accepts. Before we brush past that statement, consider the cost he paid to take our shame: *"Who for the joy set before him endured the cross, scorning its shame, and sat down at the right hand of the throne of God. Consider him who endured such opposition from sinful men, so that you will not grow weary and lose heart* (Hebrews 12:2–3).

Crucifixion was a shameful business. Its power was not only the torture, but also the disgrace it lavished on its victims. Jesus knew that soon enough a throng would gather around him, just like the one that had encircled this woman. Only instead of being shoved to the ground, he would be held up high so that everyone could join in humiliating him. There would be more gray-bearded Pharisees pointing fingers and wagging heads. There would be Roman guards fighting shamelessly for his clothes, while a pair of shameful thieves hung on his right and his left. The whole city of Jerusalem would cry out, *"Shame on you, Jesus. You wanted the shame; you got it!"*

But the Scriptures tell us that he "scorned" that shame. He accepted it freely, despite the fact that no one would be there to deflect it for him, as he had done for the adulterous woman. His mission in life was to collect the accumulated shame of mankind, to carry it up Golgotha on his back, and then to leave it there so that Paul would later write: *"As the Scripture says, 'Anyone who trusts in him will never be put to shame'"* (Romans 10:11). Did you note the condition placed there—*"Anyone who trusts in him."* I must *allow* him to take my shame.

"Who wouldn't want to give it up?" you ask. Strange though it may seem, sometimes we actually cling to our guilt and shame like a filthy blanket. We find perverse comfort in wallowing in memories of our shameful past. Those memories could lead us to giving thanks for being made new, but instead, they affirm our unworthiness. Constantly wearing this coat of shame can keep us immune to the responsibilities placed on forgiven believers. How can I possibly share my faith or stand up for the Lord when I have led such a shameful life? I'm reminded of this whenever I sing the lines from certain hymns that seem to exult in statements like "such a wretch as I."

It is essential that once shame has been acknowledged, it be released to Christ. I must trust him with my shame. Only through allowing Jesus to bear our shame are we freed to dance. Only when we are liberated from the accuser's charges can a smile replace the shame. This is not to suggest that we are sinless, but that our shame has been taken by another. And because of that, we can't keep from dancing in joyous commemoration of his gift of grace.

✦ The Dance of Repentance

But Jesus didn't stop with saving her from the stoning. His last words of instruction are important as well. *"Jesus straightened up and asked her, 'Woman, where are they? Has no one condemned you?' 'No one, sir,' she said. 'Then neither do I condemn you,' Jesus declared. 'Go now and leave your life of sin'"* (John 8:10–11).

✦

Repentance
is shame that
has learned
its lesson.

✦

Jesus had saved her from stoning, but she must now save herself from more shame. His actions were not meant to say, *"Hey, sin is no big deal. It doesn't matter how you live. It's all relative anyway!"* Those who argue against the authenticity of this passage often claim that Jesus is here portrayed as "soft on sin." Yet nothing is further from the truth. Jesus, above all others, knew what damage sin could do and what a high cost its redemption would demand. He sent the woman away, not with a moral *carte blanche*, but with a strict admonition: *"Leave your life of sin."*

Repentance is shame that has learned its lesson. When our hearts realize that the joy we thought we could find in walking away from God was a devilish mirage, we turn back to him with a renewed commitment. The shame of our sin acts as a teacher warning us not to travel that road again.

The patriarch Jacob demonstrated an education born of shame. Genesis chapter 34 recounts a period in Jacob's life when his family's immorality had become legend. After his sons killed a whole village of men because one had raped their sister, Jacob poured out his shame. *"Then Jacob said to Simeon and Levi, 'You have brought trouble on me by making me a stench to the Canaanites and Perizzites, the people living in this land.'"*

But Jacob heard the message behind the shame. When God instructed him to go back to Bethel, the place where he had begun his relationship with Yahweh, he readily went back. But first, he and his family buried the foreign idols they had carried with them. This was not buried treasure, but buried trash. He understood that in order to make a new beginning, they must leave the shame behind—*"Go now, and leave your life of sin."*

So when shame lays its steely hand on your heart, don't deny it. Acknowledge it and commit to leave behind the sin that brought it to you. But don't quit there. Give the shame to the one who takes it freely and frees the giver to dance with him. He paid its price in tears and blood. Don't let that sacrifice go unused—he died so you can dance . . . shamelessly.

*S*ome *wandered in desert wastelands,*
finding no way to a city where
they could settle.

They were hungry and thirsty,
and their lives ebbed away.

Then they cried out to the Lord in their trouble,
and he delivered them from their distress.

He led them by a straight way
to a city where they could settle.

Let them give thanks to the Lord for his
unfailing love
and his wonderful deeds for men.

✦ Psalm 107:4–8

Dancing in the Dark

When Things Go Really Wrong

"I can't do it, Daddy."

He looked up at me with one of those looks that only a six-year-old can muster: a mixture of adult embarrassment and childlike terror.

"Come on, Riley, sure you can. Just crawl through and unlock the door." He was on his hands and knees staring through the "doggydoor" into the darkness of our garage. We had gotten locked out of the house that night, and coaxing him through that little opening was my last hope before resorting to something really embarrassing—like breaking one of my own windows.

"Why don't you do it, Daddy?" He knew the answer to that: I had already demonstrated that Daddy couldn't even get his shoulders through that little hole, much less his behind. It had obviously been designed with a small dog in mind . . . or a small child. It was him or nobody. "But, Dad, it's dark in there."

The sum of all fears for a little boy is entering a darkened room, alone, at night. After all, who knew what might be lurking in there? And no matter how I tried to assure him that our garage was a "monster-free zone," he wasn't buying it. He was convinced that monsters paid little attention to "No Boogie Men Allowed" signs. In fact, there was probably a big, mean one waiting to grab him by the ankles, pull him under our family's Chevy mini-van, and do unspeakable things to him. He was about to lose his nerve and start crying, and I could see that my chances of getting back in the house without a broken window were slipping.

> ✦
>
> And no matter how I tried to assure him that our garage was a "monster-free zone," he wasn't buying it.
>
> ✦

"Riley, the light switch is right by the door. You'll be in the dark for maybe five seconds, max." I watched him mentally calculate how much damage a monster could do in five seconds. "And Son, I'll be right here," I promised.

"Are you sure?" he asked.

Now that is one of life's really *big questions.* It comes in various forms, but the bottom line is always the same:

"Will you catch me?"

"Are you gonna walk out when the going gets rough?"

"Will you love me tomorrow?"

"Can I really trust you?"

If anyone knew how to answer these queries, it was the psalmist. He understood the fears of little boys and big men who look down the dark passages of life and pray, "Father, will you see me through?" He understood the challenge of dancing in the dark, the struggle of trusting and obeying when things look bleak. So he answers the question confidently in the opening verse of Psalm 107. *"Give thanks to the Lord, for he is good; his love endures forever."*

It was a mantra that Israel would recite for generations. It was repeated in one form or another over fifty times in the psalms. It was the cornerstone of the old covenant, and it is the solid rock of the New Testament. *"For God so loved the world . . ."* It's a truth that's simple to grasp but hard to hold on to—especially in the *dark*. Whether it's a hurricane wiping out a small town or an epidemic sweeping through a large city, frightening circumstances bring out the six-year-old in us all. "Where is God when the lights go out?" we ask. "And how can I *know* that he'll stay there?"

The questions become even more troubling when the darkness is self-induced. When sin and selfishness fracture the family or blacken a reputation, the simple promise of God's ever-present faithfulness can seem awfully flimsy. After all, what kind of holy God would still love someone like me?

It is because of these nagging doubts that the 107th psalm has more than one verse. If it were sufficient just to say, "God will love you forever," the writer would have quit right there. But instead, in the following verses he gives us a brief review of God's track record of faithfulness. Like a celestial credit-rating company, he prints out God's TRW report and proves that he is worthy of our trust by reminding us of his consistent past.

And it's required reading for anyone who wants to learn how to dance in the dark.

✦ Four Snapshots of Unfailing Love

When do you most often wonder about God's love? The four scenes described in Psalm 107 span the four most common "dark places" into which doubt creeps. Each one is different, yet each is the same. One sentence is repeated in each of the sections we'll consider. It is found in verses 6, 13, 19, and 28: *"Then they cried out to the Lord in their trouble, and he delivered them from their distress."*

This assuring refrain follows all four verses of this divine love song. No matter what difficulty or disaster the psalmist describes, God brings deliverance to the distressed. It almost sounds like a children's sing-along camp song: "Second verse, same as the first!" He's still here, and he still loves you.

But let's look at each scene, because every now and then, even the most hardy among us asks: "Father, are you sure?"

When Times Are Tough

The first picture the psalmist pulls from his photo album shows some poor souls who have lost their way and are in danger of dying.

> *Some wandered in desert wastelands,*
> *finding no way to a city where they could settle.*
> *They were hungry and thirsty,*
> *and their lives ebbed away.*
>
> (Psalm 107:4–5)

Can you see the lone figure lost in the sand dunes? His mouth is parched and his belly is aching. All he can see for miles is sand, sand, and more sand. As the sun beats down on him, he realizes that if he doesn't find help soon, he'll wind up as a vulture buffet. As you look at him, remember that the writer doesn't blame this traveler for his predicament. It wasn't as though he willfully got into trouble. He just got lost.

And haven't we all? The day starts out on track, but before lunch a phone call rocks our world. A wrong decision or an odd sequence of events lands us in the emergency room or the judge's chambers. It wasn't your fault that the drunk driver chose the same road as your teenage son. It wasn't your fault that the partner who promised to be fair and square is suing you for all you're worth. It wasn't your fault that your wife won cancer's deadly lottery.

But it's your pain and your darkness. What do you do when times are tough? Job's friends counseled him to examine his life for some secret sin that must have brought on the calamity. Others suggested that he just curse God in anger and take the consequences. But the psalmist declares that God still loves you, despite what circumstances may say. The Almighty is waiting for you to call on him so he can prove that love. The wise wanderer knows what to do when lost and alone: *"Then they cried out to the Lord in their trouble . . ."*

Ironically, tough times are great for one's prayer life. There's nothing like a little financial or medical crisis to crank up your communication with God. Yet even these "foxhole" prayers are heeded by the one who promised to always love you.

> *Then they cried out to the Lord in their trouble,*
> *and he delivered them from their distress.*
> *He led them by a straight way*
> *to a city where they could settle.*
> *Let them give thanks to the Lord for his unfailing love*
> *and his wonderful deeds for men.*
>
> (Psalm 107:6–8)

Like a patient parent finding a lost child, the Lord leads the wanderer to a place of safety. The psalmist even notes that the path he leads them on is "straight" compared to the crooked trails they had become lost in. The rhythm for the whole psalm is set in this passage:

1. Trouble strikes.
2. Call out to God!
3. He brings help and hope.

But let's not leave out the last refrain: the response of the rescuees. The writer actually tells them how to respond: *"Give thanks."* They are to go from asking for help in the darkness of their desperation to "dancing in praise" of God's deliverance. The cry for help from the desert of fear and worry is only the first verse;

the chorus of thanksgiving must follow. Sadly, the first verse is all some ever sing, and they learn to sing it well. *"Oh, please, Lord, help me! I promise I'll do better next time, if you'll just get me out of this fix!"* But when the Lord's deliverance comes, the desperate victims become the forgetful redeemed. Like Israel, when we've settled into our Promised Land, the desert of Egypt becomes a distant memory. God cautioned his people against this pitfall. *"When you have eaten and are satisfied, praise the Lord your God for the good land he has given you. Be careful that you do not forget the Lord your God, failing to observe his commands, his laws and his decrees that I am giving you this day"* (Deuteronomy 8:10–11).

◆

The psalmist wants you to recall just how it felt to look sin in the eyes and say, "Okay, let's go."

◆

And the dance of thankfulness should not be rushed. Taking time to be specific in our thanks is time well spent. Our sons found this to be the case when we tried to expand their dinnertime prayer vocabulary. In the beginning, their prayers would have made Hemmingway proud: short, concise, and to the point. "Thank you God for this food and everything we have. In Christ's name, amen." They took fifteen seconds, tops. So we outlawed general phrases like "Thank you for everything" and challenged them to be more specific and thoughtful about counting their blessings. It was Riley, our six-year-old, who finally got the message—more or less. His prayer started out in the same old way "Thank you God for . . ." then came a long pause, during which I later learned he took a quick peek at the table ". . . for my milk and my corn and my mashed potatoes and gravy and my peas . . . even though I don't want any tonight."

Maybe the best rule of thumb is that our cry of thankfulness to God today should be as loud and long as our cry for deliverance was yesterday. All the better for others to hear and God's name to be praised.

When You Get Caught

The next picture is so dark that you may have to squint to make out the figure in the shadows. He's the one chained to the wall of a gloomy, stone cell. His head is bowed, his shoulders slumped, and his future is bleak. It's the look of a condemned man. While you might think he's in jail for his noble beliefs—perhaps a prophet whose willingness to stand for righteousness has landed him in Herod's holding tank—we've no such hero here. This is just a picture of your garden variety sinner, getting just what he deserves:

> *Some sat in darkness and the deepest gloom,*
> *prisoners suffering in iron chains,*
> *for they had rebelled against the words of God*
> *and despised the counsel of the Most High.*
> *So he subjected them to bitter labor;*
> *they stumbled, and there was no one to help.*
> (Psalm 107:10–12)

The language leaves little doubt that this detainee isn't here by accident. Unlike the previous group of unintentionally lost wanderers, this guy knew what he was doing. He had both *"rebelled"* against the will of God and *"despised"* divine counsel. He saw the sign, he read the rules, he knew it was wrong, and he did it anyway. No excuses, no mistake. Just plain old sin.

I would ask you if this sounds familiar, but you'd probably take the fifth. I know I would. Memories of willful disobedience to God are not my favorites. Yet getting us to remember those moments is the psalmist's goal. He wants you to reach back and recall just how it felt to look sin in the eyes and say, "Okay, let's go." What a basketful of feelings tumbles out after that: the adrenaline rush of touching the taboo and tangling with the forbidden . . . the sweaty tension of wondering if anyone was looking, if anybody noticed . . . the pit-of-the-stomach ache that comes with a "morning after" attack of morals . . . the sour taste of guilt that wells up in the wake of willful sin . . . the weight of depression and self-loathing that hidden deceit breeds . . . and finally, the continuing fear that some-day, somehow, somebody will find out.

And sometimes they never do. Sin, well buried, can stay hidden for decades. But more often, the truth does come out and the crook is caught, tripping over his own web of lies. Friends are shocked. Family is embarrassed. Enemies are elated.

But what about God? How does he feel?

Sin is serious stuff with God. It fouled up Paradise and put Christ on the cross. No fair discussion of God's loving mercy would minimize the disgusting, destructive nature of sin nor ignore the punishment God metes out. A reading of the various penalties in the Mosaic law reminds even the most grace-oriented Christian that behavior does matter to Jehovah. So the psalmist rightfully points out that God is the one who both *passes* the sen-tence and *administers* it. The prisoner is in chains because of God's judgment. Sometimes that judgment is acted out by a court of law and other times by a wounded spouse. But in each case, sin costs, and it is God alone who writes the price tag.

So, what would possess this suffering sinner to cry out to God? Visions of a loving heavenly Father are hard to maintain while being subjected to the *"bitter labor"* he brings. It's the same in the human family: As a child, I knew my father loved me, but right after a spanking wouldn't have been the time to ask me to prove it. Satan knows our tendency to question God's mercy while bumping up against his justice. He whispers in the prisoner's ear that God is the last person he should cry out to: "Why would you call for help from the same Lord who is now disciplining you? And what would God say after you got his attention? Why, he'd sound just like your mother when she caught you with your Sunday clothes covered in mud: *"Why look at you! Look at the mess you've made all because you just couldn't say no! And didn't I tell you it would come to this? But would you listen to me? . . . Noooooo. You thought you knew better. Well, mister muddy-britches, maybe next time you'll listen. Just take a good look in that mirror so you won't forget this!"*

178

"If that's what you want," Satan mocks, "then go ahead, fall on your knees and cry out to your God; but my advice is sit down and shut up."

No wonder we try to crawl away and hide when sin brings us down. If that's the kind of response we imagine from God, we'd have to be crazy to call out to him for help. But the writer stands by his first verse: *"The love of the Lord endures forever."* Even the willful sinner can dance in the dark if he will look to the Lord. And when he does, he will find grace, not disgust, in those eyes:

> *Then they cried to the Lord in their trouble,*
> *and he saved them from their distress.*
> *He brought them out of darkness and the deepest gloom*
> *and broke away their chains.*
> *Let them give thanks to the Lord for his unfailing love*
> *and his wonderful deeds for men.*
> (Psalm 107:13–15)

Once again, God inspires our thankfulness with his faithfulness. Though the chains may not break physically, countless prisoners will thank God for setting them free indeed, through his love and his son. For divine forgiveness does not mean that a human sentence will be commuted or that a spouse will gladly return. The consequences of sin can remain long after the sting of its guilt is removed. But it does mean that you can find the heart to dance—even on death row.

When Your Choices Are Foolish

Gomer Pyle. I can see him now, running behind an angry Sergeant Carter trying to explain why Sarge's dress uniform was in tatters just before the general's visit. He was the TV symbol of foolish innocence and misguided goodness. And it's his picture that we discover next in our review of God's faithful love.

> *Some became fools through their rebellious ways*
> *and suffered affliction because of their iniquities.*

179

They loathed all food
and drew near the gates of death.

(Psalm 107:17–18)

If any group deserves pity, it is this one. Unfortunately, laughter is what they most often provoke. The Hebrew term "fool" doesn't indicate brain damage or mental impairment; it describes someone who doesn't use common sense. The classic Jewish story tells it best:

> "What are you looking for down on your hands and knees?" a friend asks a fool.
> "I've lost a gold coin. Won't you help me find it?"
> "Certainly," says the friend. "Where do you think you dropped it?"
> "Over there by the synagogue."
> "Then why are you looking in front of the baker's door?"
> "Oh, the light's much better here."

Though less humorous, our choices are often just as thoughtless. We blithely feed our folly with false assurances: We can compromise our morals just a tad without getting dirty. We can get just a little involved in an extramarital affair and not do any harm. We can go to a raucous beer bash and not get into trouble or tarnish our reputation. Again and again we buy the lies: *We are in control. We know when to stop. We can handle it.*

But that's foolishness. The stacks of ruined careers and failed marriages get minimized by our Gomer-Pylism. All the while, Satan is busy placing just the right temptations in our path. Soon, we are snagged by the seductress's smooth words and brazen overtures like the "simple youth" in Proverbs chapter 7. There the writer depicts Gomer strolling down "her" street at sunset. Foolish timing. She grabs him by the collar and lays the lines on him:

> *I came out to meet you;*
> *I looked for you and have found you!*

180

I have covered my bed
>> *with colored linens from Egypt. . . .*
Come, let's drink deep of love till morning;
>> *let's enjoy ourselves with love!*
My husband is not at home;
>> *he has gone on a long journey.*
He took his purse filled with money
>> *and will not be home till full moon.*
>> >> (Proverbs 7:15–20)

What a come on! What kind of dope would buy a pitch like that? You know what kind—our kind. The fool inside us wants to believe that everybody is on the level, that if you are careful, you can play on the freeway and not get hurt. We blunder along, with a good-natured goofiness that really is convinced that a hot stove won't burn us. It's no surprise, then, that when the trap slams shut and our stupidity lands us in sin, we panic. I like the proverb writer's description:

He followed her
>> *like an ox going to the slaughter,*
like a deer stepping into a noose . . .
>> *little knowing it will cost him his life.*
>> >> (Proverbs 7:22–23)

"Shazaam! How did this happen to me?" he asks in desperate embarrassment. The answer is plain—it happened because you were foolish. But that's when the fool's reaction begins to differ from those we've looked at before. Unlike the willful sinner, the fool is so shocked by his own failings and shamed by his choices that his world caves in. All he wants is a hole to die in. Did you notice that wish in the text: *"They loathed all food and drew near the gates of death."* That's awfully beautiful language to describe an ugly act—suicide. It's the nightmare of every teenager's parents, as most of those who commit suicide are under the age of twenty. Leaving heartrending notes that describe their inner emptiness, they believe there is no hope left for them. Some join with other deluded friends in "suicide pacts" in a vain attempt to stem the loneliness of the most lonely act of all. A momentary dance with the devil becomes a death march whose last step is self-destruction.

♦

It's never too late for him to restore the prodigal who's willing to come home.

♦

Others, while avoiding physical suicide, accomplish the same thing in the spiritual realm. Convinced that they are no longer worthy of God's forgiveness, they throw off all their moral moorings and live the life of the doomed. They carve morbid tatoos into their flesh and dress in funereal colors. As one young lady put it, "With the mistakes I've made, what kind of life can I expect?" They don't just draw near the gates of death, they decide to spend the rest of their life camped there.

Don't be a fool! the psalmist shouts. You *can* live again. You can even *dance* with God. He is ready to forgive even the most foolish of sinners. If we will only be smart enough to call out to him in the darkness, he will restore hope and joy to a heart full of shame. It is this message that Christian families must embed in their children's minds. The love of the Lord endures *forever!* It's never too late for him to restore the prodigal who's willing to come home. And he will do it with the simplest of remedies.

> He sent forth his word and healed them;
> he rescued them from the grave.
> Let them give thanks to the Lord for his unfailing love
> and his wonderful deeds for men.
> (Psalm 107:20–21)

It is the truth of God that the fallen fool needs to hear: his love never fails and his divine care is always available! The word of the Lord will renew the spirit and give the former fool a song of thanks to sing . . . and even a dance or two of praise!

When Your World Falls Apart

If you haven't seen yourself in the three photos we've peered at so far, sit tight. This one's for you. The final group the psalmist describes had no need to call out to God. They were on top of the world . . . and they knew it!

> *Others went out on the sea in ships;*
> *they were merchants on the mighty waters.*
> *They saw the works of the Lord,*
> *his wonderful deeds in the deep.*
> *For he spoke and stirred up a tempest*
> *that lifted high the waves.*
> *They mounted up to the heavens and went down to the depths;*
> *in their peril their courage melted away.*
> (Psalm 107:23–26)

Who are these guys? These are the captains of high finance, the successful, the affluent. They are the well-fed yuppies and well-pensioned retirees who've thought of every eventuality and planned for every problem. Life has been good to them, and all their stocks are soaring. They haven't given way to willful sin nor have they wandered into foolish mistakes. No, they are merchants, deal makers, and yacht owners. Though they see the hand of God as they cruise the seas of life, they don't need any blessings from him—they've bought their own, thank you very much.

Before you assume that these guys are not believers, consider the realities of Western Christianity. Success and affluence are deemed by many to be a believer's right. The "name it and claim it" prophets have told us that we need only believe in God's power to bless the bank, and untold millions will be ours. Less outlandish, but just as harmful, is the notion that poverty will be kept from the door of those who are truly committed to Jesus. Now just how that can be construed from the teachings of the one who had "no place to lay his head" is a bonafide mystery. But the "deceitfulness of riches" is powerful. While I may sing "I need thee every

183

hour" on Sunday, my comfortable home and moderate savings account sing their own sweet song of security. Without realizing it, I, too, become the merchant on the mighty waters who begins to believe my sails can handle any wind.

Then comes the storm. Water swamps my decks in the form of unexpected tragedy. The market collapses, my plans go sour, or my health disintegrates. And all that swaggering courage and boasting bravado rush overboard with my dreams. *"In their peril their courage melted away."* No time for dancing now—I'm far too busy bailing water.

So why not call out to the Lord? After reading this far, one would think it was the obvious choice: "Three out of four experts agree—when in trouble, call on God." But the self-sufficient sailor doesn't think of this option at first. He is too used to believing that *"Life is what you make it"* and *"If life gives you lemons, you should make lemonade."* Calling out to God seems like failure. But has the sailor considered who brought this failure on?

The text teaches that this storm was no freak of nature; it was the hand of God. Many become uncomfortable at the thought of God actually sending calamity, but reading just a few Bible stories from Israel's history should be enough to silence that protest. Our modern notion of a Santa Claus God, who would never let bad things happen to anyone, runs afoul of a passage like this one. It was God who raised up those waves. It was God who sent the storm. And he seemed to do it for a purpose—he wanted to get Popeye's attention. He wants him to remember who really powers the ship.

And finally Popeye does remember. He calls out to the Lord. And God's response is shocking in its consistency. No recriminations. No verbal spanking. No *"Oh now you want my help!"* He just does what God does best—he loves him forever.

> *He stilled the storm to a whisper;*
> *the waves of the sea were hushed.*
> *They were glad when it grew calm,*

and he guided them to their desired haven.
Let them give thanks to the Lord for his unfailing love
and his wonderful deeds for men.
(Psalm 107:29–31)

Anyone who has ever experienced a storm at sea or a good dose of clear-air turbulence in a plane can relate to that moment. Like Jesus on the boat with his disciples, God stills the waves and brings peace. Sailors fall to their knees in thanks and make promises of renewed dependence on God . . . that they might keep for a whole week. Or maybe a month. Or even a year. But soon enough, they'll be back out there, thinking themselves the masters of their own destinies and needing to be reminded once more of who's really in charge.

And we'll be right there with them, needing to be taught again how to dance in the dark.

✦ To Dance Like a Child

So it all comes down to trust. That's what the 107th psalm is intended to prove. Our God is trustworthy even when things look bleak.

And that's the secret of dancing in the dark. It is deciding who you trust when the lights go out. It is rejecting Satan's claim that you are unworthy of even addressing God. It is the belief that God can help you live again even after you've made an absolute fool of yourself. It is ignoring the chides of Satan that you should be able to handle this on your own. It's simple, really, if we can only remember it. I have one particular memory that helps me hold on to that truth.

It was during my third-grade year that I managed to make three sixth-graders mad enough to chase me all the way home. My mouth had gotten their goat, and though they couldn't pay me back under the watchful eye of the playground attendant, there was no one to protect me once we left the school grounds. When I spotted them following me, I made a mad dash for my house, which was situated right next to the church where my father preached. Thinking I could lose them by cutting across the parking lot, I darted around the back of the church building. They must have seen that move coming, because they cut off my escape and stood in the parking lot between me and my own back door.

"Okay, Smart Mouth. What do you want to call us now?" The biggest of the three gave me a shove, and I hit my head against the block wall behind me. It smarted, but I tried not to show it. Then I noticed that my father's car was in the driveway. That meant he was probably in his study, and the study window faced the parking lot. One good yell would bring him running to my aid.

✦

He took hold of my shoulder so tightly, I thought he was about to bloody my nose.

✦

But one of the boys spotted my glance and said, "Oh look, guys, that's his house. Maybe he's gonna call his daddy! The little *baby* needs to call his daddy!" They all smirked. In that split second, logic succumbed to rage, and I waded into the three of them with my fists flying.

They cleaned my clock. When they were finished, my nose was bleeding, my shirt was torn, and my school books and papers were strewn everywhere. "Next time, maybe you'll be more polite, Smart Mouth!" With that they left, congratulating each other on the lesson they'd taught me. I picked up my things and slunk through my gate up to the back door. If I could sneak in quietly, no one would have to know of my humiliation. But as God would have it, I met my mom coming out the door with a load of laundry. "Oh, my goodness," was all she could say as she dropped the clothes basket and swept me into the kitchen. She thought I had been hit by a car. But when she got a better look at my bruises, she called for my father.

"Did you get into a fight at school?" he asked, with none of the sympathy my mother had shown.

"No sir. It was right out in the parking lot. Three sixth-graders, Dad. They followed me home." When he heard what the odds were, his faced softened.

"Why didn't you call me. I was right there?" Now it was my turn to be tough.

"I'm no sissy, Dad. I wasn't gonna call you."

All at once the firmness came back to my father's face. He took hold of my shoulder so tightly, I thought *he* was about to bloody my nose. "You listen here, Jefferson. It's never *sissy* to call your father for help, especially when it's three on one!"

Though I hadn't shed a tear through the whole ordeal, my father's words broke my resolve. As I cried, he hugged me tight, and I think I felt some water on his cheek as well. "Don't ever think you can't call me," he whispered. "That's what daddy's are for."

Need I say more?

YOU *sweep men away in the sleep of death;*
they are like the new grass of the morning—
though in the morning it springs up new,
by evening it is dry and withered.

✦ Psalm 90:5–6

Save the Last Dance for Me

Facing the Final Fight

I took a walk in a graveyard with my sons. It was a beautiful fall day, and multicolored leaves had sprinkled the graves with splashes of red and yellow. My six-year-old was mesmerized by these little scraps of natural art, but my eight-year-old was doing what he loves to do best—reading. He is at that wonderful age when reading is more a pleasure than a chore. He'll read signs in shop windows and billboard advertisements like they were treasure maps. But on this occasion he was reading headstones. We had stopped by the cemetery to see my father's grave—an odd custom, I suppose, for folks who don't believe that souls sleep in coffins. But I wanted the boys to have some connection with their past.

189

After showing them my grandparent's graves and my father's headstone, I set the them free to explore a bit. Riley went leaf collecting while Taylor walked slowly down the rows reading more grave markers. All at once he stopped at one particular stone, knelt down and touched it. I began making inner bets about what had attracted his attention—probably a child's grave marker, maybe one of those new ones that has a picture etched right in the marble. But when Taylor lingered there, kneeling motionless for a solid minute, my curiosity could no longer be reined in. I meandered close enough to see that the marker he was staring at was just a plain headstone, and though I couldn't make out the name, there didn't seem to be anything unique about it. "What did you find, Son?"

"Aw, nothing," he said without moving. It was clear he wanted this moment to remain private, so I walked away, my curiosity unquenched. I managed to wait till we were all back in the van leaving the cemetery before asking him more.

"Whose grave marker were you looking at?"

"I don't really know, Dad. But the person had my name—Taylor."

Something inside me wilted. I hadn't intended for this little family history lesson to go quite this deep. But now it had happened. My son had looked into the face of man's oldest enemy— and he had seen his own reflection.

Do you remember when you first realized that people die? Maybe it was the passing of a goldfish or family dog that unveiled the terrible secret. But it doesn't really sink in until the loss is human. An aging grandparent or great-uncle has a stroke, and within days you're dressed up in your Sunday clothes and sitting in a funeral parlor that smells of camellias and polished wood. Your father lifts you up to look into the casket, and death looks back at you from the face of a loved one. And that face looks strangely peaceful, if the embalmer has done his job well, like he's just drifted off to sleep. In fact, one of the best compliments you can pay a mortician is to say, "Aunt Judy looks so good! Why she looks like she could just sit up and talk!" But, oh boy, it would clear out the mortuary if she did. That's because she won't ever talk again in this life . . . or laugh or cry or anything. She's dead . . . and one day, you will be too. The psalmist puts it bluntly:

> *You sweep men away in the sleep of death;*
> *they are like the new grass of the morning—*
> *though in the morning it springs up new,*
> *by evening it is dry and withered.*
>
> (Psalm 90:5–6)

With that kind of comforting assurance, how can anybody dance with God? After all, if death is inescapable and the grave unavoidable, what reason for celebration exists? Death has always been one of life's grim certainties. You can ignore it; you can pretend it won't happen to you; or you can hide from the truth like the lady who promised, "I'm not going to age—I'm going to have face-lifts till my ears meet!" But just about the time you think you've dodged its black bullet, death pops up like a twisted jack-in-the-box, grinning a grave digger's smile. It stands at the end of every road like some demonic customs officer with his hand out for everything you've acquired while on your little journey here. In the end, death takes all . . . or does it?

It is God's desire that we face our own mortality with courage and confidence. Through learning to trust in God's love and Christ's grave-defeating resurrection, we can gain the knowledge that allows us to dance at our own funeral. But three myths about death must be banished so these truths can shine through.

✦ Myth #1: Death Is a Blessed Gift from God

I've heard those words spoken to bereaving loved ones who display their anger and frustration at the seemingly senseless death of a family member. They are told, "Don't be mad. God must have needed him in heaven." There's even an old hymn that used to be a favorite at funerals called "Gathering Flowers for the Master's Bouquet." It pictures the death of a saint as God plucking a beautiful flower in full bloom and taking it home with him. When a loved one dies, the song suggests, we should be comforted by knowing that God thought them worthy of his celestial bouquet. But be assured. That kind of convoluted logic is rotten to the core. To see death as God's little grim reaper, roaming the highways looking for cute souls to snatch away, and Jehovah as some kind of demented FTD in the sky is neither biblical nor comforting.

> To see Jehovah as some kind of demented FTD in the sky is neither biblical nor comforting.

Death is the seed of sin, not the gift of God. Look at James's words: *"But each one is tempted when, by his own evil desire, he is dragged away and enticed. Then, after desire has conceived, it gives birth to sin; and sin, when it is full-grown, gives birth to death"* (James 1:14–15).

Death originated with sin and will forever be connected to it. It was not chosen by God nor was it part of his original plan for mankind. That's why the Garden of Eden had no cemetery. When God formed man from the ground and breathed into him the breath of life, he was designed for eternity. Without sickness or disease to destroy his body, wouldn't man have lived forever? In fact, there is nothing in the Bible to indicate that had Adam steered clear of the fateful tree, he wouldn't have celebrated his 8,996th birthday last year! But Adam and Eve chose death. They knew the consequences and took the bite anyway. Every cemetery we drive by and every funeral we attend should remind us of the horrible results of ignoring the will of God. Yet even funerals themselves can mask this truth.

Ever consider the reason behind the traditions that accompany a burial? Why do we dress the dead in new clothes and cover the decaying flesh with makeup? Why do we spend hundreds of dollars for flowers to surround the casket as though their beauty could in some way distract from the heartbreaking loss that death almost always is? We speak of the blessed release that death brings, and sometimes when suffering has preceded death, we even describe the deceased as "getting what they wanted." And at a Christian's funeral, we can even make death sound like a great deal: No more pain, no more tears. Sign up today . . . and get your cyanide tablet at the rear of the chapel. I think not.

Death and heaven are not twin sons of the same father. Heaven is the glory of being with God. Death is the separation of man from his loved ones and his earthly life. Death does not assure heaven nor is it the only way to get there—ask the Old Testament patriarch Enoch about other travel options: the Bible says that God just "took him." While death is not the only way out, it is the one that most of us will take—but don't let anybody tell you that believers are supposed to be happy about it.

Let's make this very clear.

Nobody wants to die. It's not natural. It's not noble. It's not spiritual. The cancer-ridden friend, racked with pain, who says she wants to die is not longing for the grave, she just wants the pain to stop; and death, though undesirable, seems the only option. Even Jesus didn't run headlong into the grave's cold embrace. Knowing more than we ever will about the nature of death, he tried to talk the Father out of it—"Let this cup pass from me." Even with the glory that awaited, those were his sentiments on the subject. That's because he knew that death was an enemy of God and an ally of Satan. It was to be defeated and dethroned, not domesticated and given a place at the family table. It was to be hated and abhorred, recognized for the robber of joy that it is. Any other approach leads to irreconcilable inconsistencies in God's love and contradictions in God's Word. The Christian needn't resort to fuzzy logic and Hallmark card theology when someone asks, "Why do people die?"

Just answer honestly: the truth is that people die because of sin. God didn't want it. We don't like it. And death isn't a good deal no matter how you slice it.

So it's okay to be mad.

✦ Myth #2: Thinking about Death Will Spoil Your Life

Gallows humor has been around since man first laughed. It is our line of first defense: If we laugh at it, it won't hurt us.

"How are sales going at the new cemetery, Sam?"

"Just great, people are dying to get in!"

But be careful where you tell this kind of joke—death is still no laughing matter. Proper society and good manners tell us we shouldn't be jesting about something so serious, so most of us drop to our second line of defense: If you can't laugh at it, ignore it. We choose to combat our fear with silence. We simply don't speak of it. Even among Christians, talk of death is rare and prompted only by necessity. While discussions of how wonderful heaven will be are weekly occurrences, chats about dying somehow get bypassed.

But by sidestepping the subject, we miss an important lesson that death has to teach. Psalm 90 again sheds some light on the issue.

> *The length of our days is seventy years—*
> *or eighty, if we have the strength;*
> *yet their span is but trouble and sorrow,*
> *for they quickly pass, and we fly away.*
> *Who knows the power of your anger?*
> *For your wrath is as great as the fear that is due you.*
> *Teach us to number our days aright,*
> *that we may gain a heart of wisdom.*
>
> (vv. 10–12)

To avoid thinking about death is to tell oneself some quiet lies about life—lies like, "I've got all the time I need. I'll deal with that later."

> ✦ It is the teen who plays his way through the weekend, strategically ignoring the paper that is due on Monday.

194

+ It is the woman who watches movies till dawn in order to avoid preparing for the important meeting at 7:00 the next morning.

+ It is the businessman who can't go home at 5:00 because he spent the day reorganizing his files instead of completing the project due the next working day.

What do all of these share in common? A lack of priorities. Without clear priorities, the fun will always take precedent over the necessary and the urgent will usurp the place of the important. "Putting first things first" is the hardest task ever packed into four little words. If you can't relate to that battle, I'd like to see your blood because I question your humanity. I fight the war of priorities everyday, and am even now behind on a deadline for this chapter because . . . well . . . things just got in the way! Oh I've taken all the Time Management seminars and carry the thirty-pound "Daily Organizer" binder to prove it. But though my biceps have grown, my day is only slightly less chaotic.

And prioritizing one's day is nothing compared to prioritizing one's life! Keeping core essentials—like your relationship with God and your time with family—at the head of your "To Do" list on a week-in-week-out basis is a gargantuan task. Books on the subject fly off the shelf like free lemonade on a hot July day. But the most powerful prioritizer is right in front of us, if we will only look straight at it—death.

Though death is an enemy of God, it has a wonderful power for highlighting what's truly important. The statesman Samuel Johnson said, "It's amazing how it orders a man's thinking when he discovers he is to be hanged in a fortnight."

That's what the psalmist asks for when he calls on God to teach us to number our days. The very phrase demands that we verbalize the shocking truth: We don't have all the time in the world. Our time is finite. Our days are numbered. If we had divine knowledge, we could actually have a countdown calendar showing the number of days we have remaining. How would that be for an effective prioritizer? I don't imagine we'd get lost as easily in the mundane and unimportant when we saw those numbers plummeting into double digits. I doubt we'd put off that long-hoped-for vacation or that important conversation with a friend or family member when staring at numbers like twenty-three or fifteen in the "Days Left to Live" column.

Most of us, however, won't have the "blessing" of knowing when our time is coming. It is more likely that death will overtake us as the biblical "thief in the night." Still, God expects us to have given our life's end some thought. One of the rare times that Jesus called someone a fool was when he described a rich farmer who ignored his own death sentence. While he had planned for new barns to hold a bumper crop, he hadn't planned on dealing with death.

> I'll say to myself, "You have plenty of good things laid up for many years. Take life easy; eat, drink and be merry." But God said to him, "You fool! This very night your life will be demanded from you. Then who will get what you have prepared for yourself?" This is how it will be with anyone who stores up things for himself but is not rich toward God. (Luke 12:19–21)

He was just too busy focusing on life to think about death. But his plight should make it all the more clear that taking regular, long looks into death's dark eyes is an essential for wise living. It can provide the cold slap in the face we need to jar important values back into place.

Consider also what it would do for lethargy and complacency in evangelism. When we realize that time is of the essence, sharing our faith becomes a number-one priority. Or think about how it would motivate us to tend to relationships that need mending or wrongs that need correcting. Knowing that our days are numbered helps us avoid procrastination and take those difficult steps more quickly.

A healthy awareness of death's inevitability not only forces us to deal with the unpleasant or difficult things in life, it can also help us set aside time for life's more joyous tasks. The postoperative reactions of heart transplant patients attest to this fact. Many of the fortunate folks who have someone else's heart beating in their chests have told doctors and psychologists that life has seemed sweeter and family more important since their brush with death. They also report making a stronger effort to spend time enjoying their jobs, families, and lives. They count their blessings more often because a healthy respect for the fragility of life has made those blessings more precious. Odd as it may seem, seeing death up close improved their lives.

But surely it doesn't take open-heart surgery to get us talking about mortality with our families and remembering to count each day a gift. A doctor I know helped me get a fresh perspective without laying a scalpel on me. After a routine physical several years ago, he uncharacteristically asked me to step into his office after the exam. My worst fears were confirmed when he had me sit down for a chat. "Mr. Walling," he said gravely, "you are going to die."

A thousand things rushed through my mind: my father's cancer, the little nagging pains I had been having in my neck, the future I would surely never know, the weeks or even days that my life was being reduced to. After a moment of silence, he continued in his same tone, "But . . . so am I. So we just live on, don't we?" And then he laughed, slapped me on the back, and sent me out the door with a clean bill of health. I remember walking down the hall and promising myself I'd never go back to that quack! He could have given me a heart attack right there! But still I felt a strange relief, as though I'd been given another chance, as though a great burden had been lifted.

◆

My worst fears were confirmed when he had me sit down for a chat. "Mr. Walling, you are going to die."

◆

My doctor hadn't told me anything I didn't already know, but it was certainly a fact I hadn't spent much time pondering: I was going to die. I was perfectly healthy and absolutely terminal. I didn't have much trouble keeping my priorities straight that day. Yes, the effect wore off, but all I need do is tap back into the memory of hearing the words, "You are going to die," for my "To Do" list to get a fresh ordering!

✦ Myth #3: Death Is a Mystery We Can Never Understand

Among the few things television producers can count on to get an audience are programs promising to take the viewer "beyond the grave." Whether it's a show about contacting the dead or interviews with people who were clinically dead for three minutes and then lived to tell about it, humans have a rabid curiosity about what's on the other side of death. Even the Jews of Jesus' day started hanging around Lazarus's hoping to hear a preview of what "passing over" is like (John 12:9). Had Geraldo had a show in A.D. 30, Lazarus would have been a guaranteed guest.

But getting information on death doesn't demand a hunt through journals of the paranormal or an hour of tabloid TV. God has given us all the information we need about death right in the Bible. To the believer who stands in the embrace of God, it is not an inscrutable mystery. It is part of the dance that God invites us to, and none of the steps should be surprises. God has told us that each of us must face death. He has told us that death is a separation of our souls from our bodies and that our bodies will be reunited with our souls in a miraculous and eternal fashion. Most importantly, he has assured us that when we are away from our bodies we are not left alone.

> *For while we are in this tent, we groan and are burdened, because we do not wish to be unclothed but to be clothed with*

our heavenly dwelling, so that what is mortal may be swallowed up by life. Now it is God who has made us for this very purpose and has given us the Spirit as a deposit, guaranteeing what is to come. Therefore we are always confident and know that as long as we are at home in the body we are away from the Lord. (2 Corinthians 5:4–6)

The Spirit of God that resides within the Christian is a guarantee that we will not be left alone when we leave this body; rather, we will be "at home with the Lord" (v. 8). Christ pioneered the trip through "death's dark waters," gave us a living example of God's resurrection power, and promised us that our trip through the valley of death would be chilling but brief.

So why is it that death seems so mysterious? Could it be that we have a hard time remembering those promises? Or is it just man's natural difficulty with something we have not yet experienced. I have friends who have sworn to me that sky diving is an absolute blast . . . but you won't see me strapping on a chute anytime soon. If we allow the truth that God has revealed about death to be obscured by the things we don't know, we will end up like the twins who refused to be born. Surely you've heard of them.

Two twins were in their mother's womb. Swimming around in that dark warm sack, they could imagine no finer home. It was temperature controlled, comfortably snug, and the room service food was made to order! But after about nine months, an angel spoke to them, "Okay fellows, it's time to be born."

"Born?" one replied. "What's born?"

"Why, being born is when you come out of there and enjoy the wonderful world God has made."

"World?" the other twin said. "What's a world?"

"Why, the world is a marvelous place full of trees and mountains, streams and oceans. It's filled with beautiful colors and fantastic sights," the patient angel replied.

"Mountains?" one twin asked.

"Streams?" the other chimed in. After a quick consultation they told the angel, "We've never seen any of those things. We'll just stick with what we've got. We like it here just fine. We'll pass on the 'born' thing, but thanks just the same."

"Look guys," the angel said firmly, "this isn't an option. You can't stay in there. You have to be born."

"We have to?" they whined. "Will it hurt?"

"Yes, a little, I'm afraid, and you'll have to go through that dark passage beneath you, but I promise you'll be glad when it's over."

"Oooooh no. We're not going through that passage," they stubbornly replied.

"No choice guys. It's time!" And the process began.

"Please, noooo."

They cried and fought the whole way out into the world, but with their first breath of air and their first taste of mother's milk, they said, "Hey, this place is great. Why didn't you tell us it was like this?"

"I tried," the tired angel said, "but you wouldn't listen!"

◆

> With their first breath of air and their first taste of mother's milk, they said, "Hey, this place is great."

◆

Seventy years later she came to the twins again.

"Okay, fellows, it's time to die."

"Die?" they said. "What's dying like?"

"Oh, you'll be going to a wonderful place full of cherubim and archangels."

"I haven't ever seen an archangel . . . or a cherubim!" one twin snapped.

"Yeah, we like it here on earth," the second agreed. "There are mountains and streams, oceans and trees. We're quite happy here. We'll pass on this 'death' thing, but thanks anyway."

"Guys, you don't have a choice. Whether you want to or not, you're going to die. And before you ask, yes, it may hurt a little. You'll go through that grave right there beneath you."

"Grave!?" one screamed.

"Hurt!?" the other moaned.

And though they begged and pleaded and hung on to life for all they were worth, they died and went to be with the Lord. And after a moment—which was an eternity—in the presence of God and all his glory, they said to the angel, "Hey, why didn't you tell us it was this wonderful?"

"I tried," the angel said smiling, "but you wouldn't listen."

Admittedly, the last dance is one you don't get to practice for. You can only dance it with God once. But don't join those who've stopped dancing with God because they are so worried about that last dance. God knows how to dance life's final dance well enough to lead a beginner through it. So don't let Satan keep you fretting that the next tune the heavenly orchestra swings into will be "The Party's Over." They never play that song, anyway, because with him, the celebration is always just beginning.

Let the band play on!

And the Dance Goes On

The prophet was tired—bone tired. With the Almighty's help he had brought fire from heaven, ended the drought, and nuked the prophets of Baal—it had been a busy day. He had danced with God until his feet ached and his sides burned. But he had also made Queen Jezebel mad enough to lose the little religion she had. In her anger, she had sworn to see Elijah dead, and Jezebel was not a woman of idle threats.

So he did what any sensible man would do: he went to a quiet place and lay down to die. He was through with dancing, praising, and anything else that took more energy than breathing. "Stop the music!" he pleaded. "I can't dance any more!" That's not *exactly* what he said, but it's awfully close: *"I have had enough, Lord,"* he said. *"Take my life; I am no better than my ancestors"* (1 Kings 19:4). What do you know—even prophets get the blues!

But God wasn't finished with him yet. Elijah soon found himself standing in front of a cave on Mount Horeb, waiting for his appointment with Jehovah. It's a scene worth noting, for we will all stand in his sandals sometime. No matter how joyous and delightful my waltz with God may be today, tomorrow may bring hassles and heartache. I'll get tired, disappointed, or frustrated; and like Elijah, I'll just want to quit. The Word of God warns against growing "weary in well doing." Even praising God, it seems, can wear one out.

So what do you do when you're tired of dancing?

God gave Elijah some needed "prophet therapy" to get him back into the dance of life. As we finish our time together, it might be good for us to take the prophet's medicine as well.

> The Lord said, "Go out and stand on the mountain in the presence of the Lord, for the Lord is about to pass by." Then a great and powerful wind tore the mountains apart and shattered the rocks before the Lord, but the Lord was not in the wind. After the wind there was an earthquake, but the Lord was not in the earthquake. After the earthquake came a fire, but the Lord was not in the fire. And after the fire came a gentle whisper.... Then a voice said to him, "What are you doing here, Elijah?" (1 Kings 19:11–13)

Though earthquake, fire, wind, and storm passed by, the Lord was not there. But then, in a still, small voice, God spoke to the tired prophet and asked him the sixty-four thousand dollar question: "What are you doing here, Elijah?"

God renewed his danced-out servant by reminding him of two things. And I need these same reminders. First, I need him to remind me of just how big he is. Larger than my hurts. Bigger than my fears. Tougher than my temptations. He is too small to be caged in an earthquake or confined to a whirlwind. He is the one and only God. He is the definition of awesome, the picture of supreme power. When something else impresses me with its greatness, I need only remember that he created the entire universe with nothing more than a word. Though creation is sometimes called his "handiwork," God made the whole thing with just his voice.

Second, I need him to remind me of my purpose: "Why are you here, Jeff? To achieve some personal goal? To win a celestial dance contest? To snag a medal or a prize or an honor . . . ? Or are you here to glorify me by trusting my grace and simply dancing in joyous response?"

Just as God sent Elijah out with a new spark and a renewed purpose, so he fills us with refreshment and resolve. We dance not to fill the floor but to respond to God's love. We must hear him say, "There are people to be loved, hearts to be healed, and lives to be blessed. Go serve me . . . and smile while you do!"

So be prepared. The dance we've discussed is an unending one—thrilling at times, mild at moments, but never coming to a halt. It continues around his throne forever, in a celestial ballroom big enough for all the saints throughout the ages to celebrate his love forever.

Well, I've enjoyed our little chat about dancing, but the time for talking is over. The band is tuned up, the dance floor is cleared, and your heavenly partner is waiting.

Let the dance continue . . .

and continue . . .

and continue!